Java Spring Framework
100 Interview Questions

X.Y. Wang

Contents

5 Expert 131

Chapter 1

Introduction

Welcome to "Java Spring Framework: 100 Interview Questions". This book is designed to help you prepare for interviews and deepen your understanding of the Spring Framework, one of the most popular and widely-used frameworks in the Java ecosystem. Over the past few years, Spring has become an essential tool for developers building enterprise-level applications, web services, and microservices. With its comprehensive set of features, Spring has made it easier for developers to work with various technologies while maintaining a consistent and modular architecture.

This book is divided into five sections, starting with basic concepts and progressing through to advanced topics and expert-level challenges. Each section contains a set of questions that are designed to test your understanding of various aspects of the Spring Framework, including its core modules, dependency injection, aspect-oriented programming, data access, web development, and more. These questions will not only help you prepare for interviews but also deepen your understanding of the framework and its best practices.

Section 1: Basic - This section contains essential questions about the Spring Framework, such as its core modules, the inversion of control (IoC) container, dependency injection, and more. These questions will help you build a solid foundation in Spring and understand its fundamental concepts.

Section 2: Intermediate - This section delves deeper into various aspects of the Spring Framework, including bean scopes, transaction management, Spring MVC, Spring Boot, and more. These questions will help you understand the intricacies of the framework and how its components work together.

Section 3: Advanced - In this section, you will explore advanced topics such as Spring AOP, Spring Data, Spring Security, and Spring Cloud. These questions will help you gain a deeper understanding of the framework and its advanced features, as well as how to apply them in real-world applications.

Section 4: Expert - This section is designed for experienced Spring developers and contains questions on advanced topics such as ApplicationContext hierarchy, Spring AOP internals, distributed transactions, and more. These questions will challenge your knowledge of the framework and help you develop expertise in using Spring effectively.

Section 5: Guru - The final section of the book is dedicated to mastering Spring and covers advanced topics such as custom namespace handlers, CQRS and event sourcing, reactive programming, and more. These questions will test your understanding of the most advanced aspects of the Spring ecosystem and help you become a true Spring guru.

With a comprehensive set of questions ranging from basic to guru-level, this book is an invaluable resource for developers looking to sharpen their knowledge of the Spring Framework. We hope that "Java Spring Framework 100 Interview Questions" will help you succeed in your interviews, advance your career, and become a better Spring developer.

Chapter 2

Basic

2.1 What is the Java Spring Framework, and why is it used?

The Java Spring Framework is a popular open-source application framework used to build dynamic and robust enterprise-level applications. It provides developers with a set of tools and techniques for developing scalable, modular, and maintainable applications in the Java programming language.

The Spring framework is widely used because it simplifies the development process and saves time and effort for developers. It offers a number of features and benefits that make it an ideal choice for building enterprise applications. Some of the key benefits of the Spring Framework are:

1. Inversion of Control (IoC) - The Spring Framework uses the concept of IoC, which allows developers to write code that is

loosely coupled and easy to maintain. With IoC, the framework is responsible for creating and managing objects, and can inject dependencies into a class, rather than creating them yourself.

2. Dependency Injection (DI) - Spring makes use of DI, which allows you to specify the dependencies of your application in the configuration files. This makes it easier to manage dependencies and ensures that your code is modular and reusable.

3. Aspect-Oriented Programming (AOP) - AOP is a programming paradigm that allows you to separate cross-cutting concerns, such as logging, security, and caching, from the main application logic. Spring supports AOP and provides developers with tools for implementing it.

4. Modularity - Spring provides a modular architecture that allows you to choose only the modules that you need. This makes it easy to scale your application and maintain a clean codebase.

5. Integration - Spring offers integration with other popular technologies and frameworks, such as Hibernate, JPA, Apache Struts, and many more. This makes it easy to use Spring with your existing stack and to integrate new technologies as they emerge.

Overall, the Java Spring Framework is an excellent choice for developing enterprise applications due to its flexibility, scalability, and modularity. With its wide range of features, Spring provides developers with the tools and techniques needed to build robust, high-performance applications.

2.2   Explain the core modules of the Spring Framework.

The Spring Framework is a powerful and versatile Java framework that provides developers with a wide range of features and tools for building robust and scalable applications. The Spring Framework is modular, which means that it is composed of several tightly integrated modules, each of which provides a specific set of features and functionality. Here are the core modules of the Spring Framework:

1. Spring Core: This module is the heart of the Spring Framework and provides basic features such as dependency injection and inversion of control (IOC). Spring Core includes the BeanFactory and ApplicationContext, which are responsible for managing Java objects and their dependencies.

2. Spring AOP (Aspect-Oriented Programming): This module provides support for aspect-oriented programming, which allows developers to modularize cross-cutting concerns like logging, caching, and security. This module is built on top of the Spring Core module and uses the same dependency injection mechanisms.

3. Spring JDBC: This module provides support for JDBC (Java Database Connectivity) and simplifies the process of working with databases. Spring JDBC includes features like the JdbcTemplate class for executing SQL statements, connection pooling, and transaction management.

4. Spring ORM (Object-Relational Mapping): This module provides support for ORM frameworks like Hibernate, JPA, and MyBatis. Spring ORM simplifies the process of integrat-

ing these frameworks into a Spring application and provides additional features like transaction management and exception handling.

5. Spring Web: This module provides support for building web applications using Spring MVC (Model-View-Controller) architecture. Spring Web includes features like request handling, view rendering, and form handling.

6. Spring Test: This module provides support for testing Spring applications using JUnit or TestNG. Spring Test includes features like mock objects, integration testing, and test context management.

These are the core modules of the Spring Framework that provide developers with a wide range of features and tools for building robust and scalable applications. By understanding these modules, developers can leverage the power of Spring to build better applications faster.

2.3   What is the Spring IoC container? How does it work?

The Spring IoC (Inversion of Control) container is the core component of the Spring Framework, responsible for managing and wiring objects in a Spring-based application. It is responsible for creating, initializing, and wiring objects defined in your application's configuration files or classes, and then making them available to other components in your application.

The Spring IoC container follows the principle of Inversion of Control, which means that instead of the developer writing code to create objects and manage dependencies, the container takes responsibility for these tasks. This approach greatly reduces the complexity of application development, allowing developers to focus on business logic rather than object creation and management.

The Spring IoC container uses a set of configuration files or annotations (such as @Component, @Autowired, or @Bean) to define the objects and their dependencies. These configuration files or annotations are processed by the container to create, configure and wire the objects together, creating the object graph of your application's components.

The Spring IoC container uses two main types of wiring to manage dependencies: constructor injection, and setter injection. With constructor injection, the container provides the necessary dependencies to the constructor of each object as it creates it. With setter injection, the container provides the necessary dependencies by calling the appropriate setter method on each object.

For example, consider the following Spring application context configuration XML file that defines a simple bean named 'myBean':

```
<beans>
    <bean id="myBean" class="com.example.MyBean">
        <property name="myDependency" ref="myDependencyBean"/>
    </bean>

    <bean id="myDependencyBean" class="com.example.MyDependency"/>
</beans>
```

In this example, the Spring IoC container creates an instance of 'MyBean', and injects into it an instance of 'MyDependency'. The 'MyBean' class might look something like this:

```
public class MyBean {
    private MyDependency myDependency;

    public void setMyDependency(MyDependency myDependency) {
        this.myDependency = myDependency;
    }
}
```

When the 'MyBean' instance is created by the Spring IoC container, it automatically calls the 'setMyDependency' method and passes in the 'MyDependency' instance, wiring the dependency and completing the object graph.

In summary, the Spring IoC container is a crucial component of the Spring Framework that uses configuration files or annotations to manage object creation, initialization, and wiring, freeing developers from having to manage these tasks themselves.

2.4   What is Dependency Injection, and what are the different types of Dependency Injection supported by Spring?

Dependency Injection (DI) is a software design pattern that promotes loose coupling between the components of an application by allowing components to be loosely coupled and only dependent on abstractions, removing the need for them to be dependent on each other.

In simple terms, DI allows one object to be supplied to another object, which requires it for its functionality. This approach enables better decoupling between classes, making them more maintainable, testable, and reusable.

Spring offers three types of Dependency Injection or IOC:

1. Constructor-based DI: Spring injects dependencies through a constructor. It requires that all required dependencies be available when an object is created. This approach is particularly useful when the object being created requires several dependencies to work.

Example:

```
public class MyController {
    private final MyService myService;

    public MyController(MyService myService) {
        this.myService = myService;
    }

    // methods
}
```

2. Setter-based DI: Spring uses the setter method to inject dependencies into an application. Setter-based DI is suitable for optional dependencies that can have a default or no value.

Example:

```
public class MyController {
    private MyService myService;

    public void setMyService(MyService myService) {
        this.myService = myService;
    }

    // methods
}
```

3. Field-based DI: In this approach, Spring injects dependencies directly into fields, which eliminates the need for setter methods or constructors. Field-based DI is suitable for small applications and allows for a cleaner and less verbose code.

Example:

```
public class MyController {
   @Autowired
   private MyService myService;

   // methods
}
```

Overall, Spring's Dependency Injection offers different options
for configuring and managing dependencies, depending on the
requirements of each component. It allows for flexible and modular app development, promoting easy testing and maintenance.

2.5   What are Spring Beans, and how are they defined?

In Spring Framework, a bean is an object that is managed
by the Spring IoC container. It is simply a Java object that
is instantiated, assembled, and otherwise managed by Spring
Framework's IoC container. Essentially, the bean is the fundamental building block of any Spring-based application.

Beans are defined in the Spring Framework using Java configuration or XML-based configuration. Java configuration involves the use of Java classes annotated with '@Configuration'
and '@Bean' annotations, while XML configuration involves the
use of a Spring XML configuration file to define beans.

Here is an example of defining a bean using Java configuration:

```
@Configuration
public class MyConfiguration {

    @Bean
    public MyBean myBean() {
        return new MyBean();
    }
}
```

In this example, 'MyBean' is a simple Java class, and the 'my-Bean' method is annotated with '@Bean', which tells Spring that this method returns a bean object that should be managed by the container.

Here is an example of defining beans using XML configuration:

```
<beans>
    <bean id="myBean" class="com.example.MyBean"/>
</beans>
```

In this example, the 'id' attribute identifies the name of the bean, and the 'class' attribute specifies the fully-qualified class name of the bean that will be instantiated.

Once a bean is defined, it can be accessed by other beans in the same container or by application code that uses the container. During runtime, the Spring IoC container is responsible for creating instances of beans, managing their lifecycle, and providing them to other parts of the application as needed.

2.6 What is the role of the application-Context.xml file in Spring?

The 'applicationContext.xml' file plays a critical role in the Spring Framework by defining the beans that make up a Spring application context. In essence, its the configuration file that defines the application context.

The 'applicationContext.xml' file contains details about the various beans that Spring can instantiate, wire together, and manage. It acts as the central hub for the Spring container and provides a way to organize and configure your beans in a flexible and modular way.

Here are some of the key elements that can be defined within the 'applicationContext.xml' file:

1. Bean definitions: The file contains bean definitions for the various objects that make up the application. Different types of bean definitions can be used to create these objects, such as a 'constructor-arg' for method parameters and 'property' for setter injections.

2. Configuration properties: The file also contains configuration properties that are used to configure various aspects of the Spring container, such as the default scope of beans or the location of other configuration files.

3. Interceptors: Spring allows you to define interceptors that can be used to add custom behavior to method calls. These interceptors can also be defined in the 'applicationContext.xml' file.

4. Life-cycle hooks: Spring offers a number of great callbacks that can be used to receive notifications during the construction and destruction of a bean. These hooks can be used to initialize or destroy a bean.

Here is an example of an 'applicationContext.xml' file:

```
<beans xmlns="http://www.springframework.org/schema/beans"
       xmlns:xsi="http://www.w3.org/2001/XMLSchema-instance"
       xsi:schemaLocation="http://www.springframework.org/schema/
           beans
        http://www.springframework.org/schema/beans/spring-beans-4.3.
           xsd">

    <bean id="myBean" class="com.example.MyBean">
        <property name="name" value="John Doe"/>
    </bean>

    <bean id="myOtherBean" class="com.example.MyOtherBean">
```

```
        <property name="someBean" ref="myBean"/>
    </bean>

</beans>
```

This example defines two beans, 'myBean' and 'myOtherBean', and specifies that 'myOtherBean' should reference 'myBean' as a property named 'someBean'. These beans can then be instantiated and managed by the Spring container.

In conclusion, the 'applicationContext.xml' file is a critical file in the Spring Framework that defines and configures the beans that are used in a Spring application context. It is an essential tool for organizing and configuring the application context in a flexible and modular way.

2.7 What is Spring AOP, and how does it differ from traditional OOP?

Spring AOP (Aspect-Oriented Programming) is a technique used in the Spring Framework to separate cross-cutting concerns from the core business logic of an application. In traditional OOP (Object-Oriented Programming), the focus is on dividing an application into independent and modular objects that work together to perform a task. However, certain concerns such as security, logging, and transaction management can span across multiple objects and can be difficult to manage.

Spring AOP addresses this issue by allowing developers to define aspects that cut across multiple objects to enforce these concerns. An aspect is a modular unit of behavior that can be applied to multiple objects consistently. AOP provides a way to define aspects and weave them into the application at runtime.

In traditional OOP, all method calls and objects are tightly coupled, meaning the method call occurs directly on the object. In Spring AOP, the responsibility of an object is only to implement the core business logic to achieve its goal, which makes objects loosely coupled. The cross-cutting concerns like transaction management, logging, and security are handled by Aspects which are then woven around objects.

Let's take the example of authentication in a web application. Instead of implementing an authentication check in every method of every object that requires authentication, an aspect can be defined that checks for authentication before executing the method. This reduces the amount of repetitive code and makes the code easier to maintain.

Spring AOP also differs from traditional OOP in that it is dynamic and applied at runtime, whereas typical object-oriented programming is static and applied at compile-time. This means that aspects can be added, removed, or modified without changing the source code of the underlying application.

In summary, Spring AOP is a technique used in the Spring Framework that allows developers to separate cross-cutting concerns from the core business logic of an application, making code more modular, reusable, and easier to maintain.

2.8 What is a Spring Aspect, and how is it used?

A Spring Aspect is a modular, cross-cutting concern in the Spring Framework that can be applied declaratively to any Spring-managed bean. As its name suggests, an Aspect is responsible for defining additional behavior that can be applied to a Spring application at runtime.

Aspects are used to implement cross-cutting concerns (i.e., functionality that is applied across multiple layers of an application) in a modular fashion. This allows developers to separate concerns such as logging, caching, and security from the core business logic of an application.

Spring Aspects are implemented using the AspectJ language, which is a powerful aspect-oriented programming (AOP) language that provides a rich set of features for defining and applying aspects. AspectJ provides support for pointcuts (which define where an Aspect should be applied), advice (which provides the behavior of the Aspect), and other AOP concepts.

To use an Aspect in a Spring application, you need to first configure the AspectJ runtime. You can then define your Aspect as a Spring-managed bean and apply it to other beans using pointcuts.

Here's an example of a simple logging Aspect that can be applied to any method in a Spring-managed bean:

```
@Aspect
public class LoggingAspect {

    @Before("execution(*␣com.example.*.*(..))")
    public void logMethodCall(JoinPoint joinPoint) {
        String methodName = joinPoint.getSignature().getName();
```

```
        System.out.println("Method called: " + methodName);
    }

}
```

In this example, the Aspect is defined as a Spring-managed
bean using the '@Aspect' annotation. It defines a single advice
method named 'logMethodCall', which is executed before any
method call in the 'com.example' package.

To apply this Aspect to a Spring-managed bean, you would
need to define a pointcut that matches the methods you want
to log:

```
@Component
public class MyService {

    public void doSomething() {
        // ...
    }

    public void doSomethingElse() {
        // ...
    }

}


@Aspect
public class LoggingAspect {

    @Before("execution(* com.example.MyService.*(..))")
    public void logMethodCall(JoinPoint joinPoint) {
        String methodName = joinPoint.getSignature().getName();
        System.out.println("Method called: " + methodName);
    }

}
```

In this example, the Aspect is applied to the 'MyService' bean
by defining a pointcut that matches any method call on the
'MyService' class. When the 'doSomething' or 'doSomethin-
gElse' method is called, the logging advice in the Aspect will
be executed before the method call.

2.9 What is Spring JDBC, and how does it simplify database operations?

Spring JDBC is a part of the Spring Framework that simplifies database operations in Java applications. It provides a JDBC-abstraction layer that eliminates the need for low-level JDBC coding and boilerplate code. Spring JDBC provides a simpler and more concise method of interacting with a database, making it much easier to manage and maintain both small and large scale database systems.

One of the main ways that Spring JDBC simplifies database operations is through the use of JDBC templates. These templates are higher-level abstractions above the JDBC APIs, which encapsulate repetitive boilerplate code and enable you to use type-safe queries. JDBC templates allow you to execute SQL statements, such as SELECT, INSERT, UPDATE, and DELETE, with fewer lines of code than would be required using raw JDBC.

Additionally, Spring JDBC's SQL exceptions are easier to handle, making it easier to provide appropriate error messages and logging. By using Spring JDBC's data access exception hierarchy, you can handle exceptions more efficiently and make your error messages more meaningful to the end user.

Another way that Spring JDBC simplifies database operations is by taking care of connection management. With Spring JDBC, you don't have to worry about opening and closing database connections manually. Instead, Spring JDBC manages your database connections efficiently using connection pools, which provide better performance and scalability for your applications.

Here's an example of how Spring JDBC simplifies database operations:

```java
// Without Spring JDBC
try {
    Class.forName("com.mysql.jdbc.Driver");
    Connection con = DriverManager.getConnection(
        "jdbc:mysql://localhost:3306/mydatabase", "myusername", "
            mypassword");
    Statement stmt = con.createStatement();
    ResultSet rs = stmt.executeQuery("SELECT * FROM mytable");
    while (rs.next()) {
        System.out.println(rs.getString("column1"));
    }
    con.close();
} catch (SQLException e) {
    // handle exception
} catch (ClassNotFoundException e) {
    // handle exception
}

// With Spring JDBC
JdbcTemplate jdbcTemplate = new JdbcTemplate(dataSource);
List<String> results = jdbcTemplate.queryForList("SELECT column1
    FROM mytable", String.class);
for (String result : results) {
    System.out.println(result);
}
```

As you can see, with Spring JDBC, there's no need to manually load the JDBC driver, open a connection, create a statement, and handle exceptions. Instead, you use the JdbcTemplate to query the database, with connection management and error handling being taken care of by the framework. This not only simplifies your code but also reduces errors and makes your application more efficient.

2.10   How does Spring support transaction management?

Spring provides comprehensive support for transaction management through the use of its transaction abstraction layer. This abstraction layer enables Spring to support declarative transaction management and programmatic transaction management.

Declarative transaction management is where transactional concerns are expressed using annotations or XML configuration, rather than being coded directly into individual Java methods. This approach is far more maintainable than directly coding transactional concerns into each individual method, and makes it far easier to adjust transactional behaviors. Spring supports declarative transaction management through the use of annotations such as @Transactional or through the use of XML configuration files.

Programmatic transaction management, on the other hand, allows developers to write code that specifies transaction boundaries explicitly. This approach is useful in more complex scenarios where fine-grained control over transaction management is required. Spring supports programmatic transaction management through the use of the TransactionTemplate and transaction manager abstraction.

Spring has support for different transaction managers and APIs like JTA, Hibernate, JPA, and JDBC. A transaction manager handles the transaction lifecycle and coordination by communicating with the underlying data source. Spring provides several built-in transaction managers like DataSourceTransactionManager, JpaTransactionManager, HibernateTransactionManager for different APIs. Spring Framework allows custom transac-

tion manager implementations to be integrated using its TransactionManager interface.

Here's an example of how to use @Transactional annotation in
Spring to enable declarative transaction management:

```
@Service
public class SomeService {

    private final UserRepository userRepository;
    private final ItemRepository itemRepository;

    @Autowired
    public SomeService(UserRepository userRepository, ItemRepository
        itemRepository) {
      this.userRepository = userRepository;
      this.itemRepository = itemRepository;
    }

    @Transactional
    public void updateAccountWithNewItems(User user, List<Item>
        items) {
      userRepository.save(user);

      for (Item item : items) {
          itemRepository.save(item);
      }
    }
}
```

In the above example, the @Transactional annotation is used to
specify that the updateAccountWithNewItems() method should
be executed within a transactional context. If any error occurs
during the execution of this method, the transaction will be
rolled back, meaning that all changes made within the transaction will be discarded.

Overall, Spring's support for transaction management in enterprise applications greatly reduces the effort involved in writing
and maintaining robust, transactional code. Developers can
choose from declarative or programmatic styles of transaction
management, and can also take advantage of Spring's support
for different transaction managers and APIs.

2.11 What is Spring MVC, and how is it different from traditional servlet-based web applications?

Spring MVC is a web framework built on top of the core Spring Framework that provides a model-view-controller (MVC) architecture for building web applications. It is designed to make it easier to build robust, scalable, and flexible web applications based on the Java language.

Compared to traditional servlet-based web applications, Spring MVC provides several advantages. Here are a few:

1. Separation of concerns: Spring MVC promotes a clear separation of concerns between the different components of a web application (such as the controller, model, and view), allowing developers to focus on one aspect of the application at a time.

2. Testability: Because Spring MVC applications are built using loosely coupled components, they are highly testable. This means that developers can write automated tests for individual components and easily test the application as a whole.

3. Flexibility: Spring MVC provides a flexible architecture that can be easily extended to support new features or integrations with other technologies or APIs.

4. Easy to use: The Spring MVC framework is designed to be easy to use and to reduce the amount of boilerplate code that developers need to write. This makes it faster and easier to build web applications.

Here's an example of how Spring MVC works:

1. A user makes a request to a Spring MVC controller, either by clicking a link or submitting a form.

2. The controller receives the request and interacts with the data model to retrieve data or perform business logic.

3. The controller then passes the data to the view, which renders the response and sends it back to the user's browser.

Overall, Spring MVC is a powerful and flexible web framework that offers many advantages over traditional servlet-based applications. Its modular design, ease of use, and testability make it a popular choice for building modern Java web applications.

2.12   What is a DispatcherServlet, and how does it work in Spring MVC?

In Spring MVC, a DispatcherServlet is the front controller that handles all incoming requests and sends them to the appropriate handler methods that can process the requests. The DispatcherServlet is the entry point of any Spring web application and is responsible for managing the life cycle of the entire application context as well as the web application context.

When a user makes a request, the DispatcherServlet receives the request and forwards it to a specialized controller that handles the specific request. The DispatcherServlet takes the request and uses its internal HandlerMapping to map the request to the proper handler. This is based on the URI and any parameters that were included in the request.

Once the handler is determined, the DispatcherServlet passes the request to the handler through its internal HandlerAdapter. The HandlerAdapter is capable of working with any handler method that is defined and registered within the application context. The handler then processes the request and returns the result to the DispatcherServlet.

The result that's returned by the handler can be of different types, it could be a view name, a Model and View Object (MAV), or even a redirect instruction. The DispatcherServlet then sends the response to the associated view resolver where it's rendered and sent back to the client.

Furthermore, the DispatcherServlet can also be configured with various other handlers like Interceptors, which are executed before and after processing the handler method. They can be used to perform pre-processing and post-processing tasks.

Overall, the DispatcherServlet acts as the central hub that manages the entire request-processing lifecycle in Spring MVC. It provides numerous out-of-the-box benefits such as mapping and handling many different types of requests and responses, working with different controllers and handlers, and handling errors in a systematic way, to name a few.

2.13 Explain the role of WebApplication-Context in Spring MVC.

WebApplicationContext is a specific implementation of the ApplicationContext interface provided by Spring Framework that serves as the container for the Spring MVC web application. It provides all the services of the ApplicationContext interface customized for use in a web application context, such as support for loading resources using relative paths, included or overridden files, ServletContext parameters, etc.

The main role of the WebApplicationContext is to provide a centralized location for managing beans and their dependencies in a web-based environment. It acts as a central hub that maintains and controls the configuration, initialization, and disposal of all beans in the Spring MVC application.

In Spring MVC, the WebApplicationContext is loaded by the DispatcherServlet when it is initialized. The DispatcherServlet creates the WebApplicationContext by reading the configuration files and registering the beans defined in them. The WebApplicationContext can also be loaded programmatically, using the ContextLoaderListener, which initializes the ApplicationContext before the DispatcherServlet.

The WebApplicationContext provides beans related to web infrastructure such as controllers, ViewResolvers, exception resolvers, handler mappings, and interceptors. It also provides beans for data access, business logic, and service layers. By organizing the beans in a single context and maintaining them in a consistent state, the WebApplicationContext ensures that all objects in the application have access to the necessary services, making them easy to manage, update, and maintain.

For example, suppose we have a Spring MVC application with two controllers, one that responds to GET requests and another that responds to POST requests. We can define both controllers in a single WebApplicationContext, and both controllers can share resources such as a data access object or a service class. By doing so, the WebApplicationContext provides a cohesive and decoupled codebase, where each part of the application has its own responsibilities and can be updated and tested independently.

In summary, the WebApplicationContext plays a crucial role in

Spring MVC application development, as it provides a centralized container for managing beans and promoting a modular, scalable architecture that improves application performance, reliability, and maintainability.

2.14 What are the differences between @Controller and @RestController annotations in Spring MVC?

The main difference between '@Controller' and '@RestController' annotations in Spring MVC is in the way they handle the HTTP response body.

'@Controller' annotation is used to create a Spring MVC controller class that is responsible for handling incoming HTTP requests. It usually handles the request and prepares the response by returning a view name, which is then resolved by a view resolver. In this way, the '@Controller' annotation is used to manage the flow of views in a Spring MVC application.

On the other hand, '@RestController' annotation is used to create a class that provides a RESTful web service. It behaves like a combination of the '@Controller' and '@ResponseBody' annotations, i.e., it handles the incoming request and returns the data directly to the client, without the need of a view resolver.

'@RestController' annotations ensure that the response body is serialized directly to the HTTP response in a format such as JSON or XML, without a view. This approach is particularly useful for building APIs that communicate in a standard format like JSON or XML.

For example, consider the following code snippet:

```
@Controller
public class MyController {

    @GetMapping("/greeting")
    public String greeting() {
        return "Hello,␣world!";
    }
}
```

In this code snippet, the '@Controller' annotation is used to create a controller class that handles incoming GET requests to the '/greeting' URL path. The method 'greeting()' prepares a view named 'Hello, world¡ which is resolved by a view resolver to render the final response.

On the other hand, consider the following code snippet:

```
@RestController
public class MyRestController {

    @GetMapping("/greeting")
    public String greeting() {
        return "Hello,␣world!";
    }
}
```

In this code snippet, the '@RestController' annotation is used to create a RESTful web service that handles incoming GET requests to the '/greeting' URL path. The method 'greeting()' returns a String "Hello, world!", which is directly serialized and sent as the response body in the format requested by the client.

In summary, the use of '@Controller' or '@RestController' depends on the nature of your web application - if you are building an API, it is better to use the '@RestController' annotation, while if you are building a web application that uses views, it is better to use the '@Controller' annotation.

2.15 How does Spring handle form submissions using the @ModelAttribute annotation?

In Spring, @ModelAttribute annotation is used to bind form data to a model object. When this annotation is used, Spring automatically maps the HTTP request parameters to corresponding fields of a model class.

To handle form submissions using @ModelAttribute annotation, we need to follow these steps:

1. Create a form in HTML or JSP page with input fields that match the fields of our model class.

```
<form action="processForm" method="post">
    <label for="name">Name:</label>
    <input type="text" id="name" name="name"><br>

    <label for="email">Email:</label>
    <input type="email" id="email" name="email"><br>

    <label for="message">Message:</label>
    <textarea id="message" name="message"></textarea><br>

    <input type="submit" value="Submit">
</form>
```

2. Create a model class with fields that match the form fields.

```
public class ContactForm {
    private String name;
    private String email;
    private String message;

    // getters and setters
}
```

3. In the Spring controller, handle the form submission with a @PostMapping method.

```
@PostMapping("/processForm")
public String processForm(@ModelAttribute("contactForm") ContactForm
    contactForm) {
  // do something with the contactForm object
  return "successPage";
}
```

4. In the @PostMapping method, we use @ModelAttribute annotation to bind the form data to a model object. The attribute name is optional and is used to give a name to the model object.

5. Spring automatically maps the form fields to the corresponding fields of the ContactForm object. We can access these fields using getter methods.

6. Do something with the contactForm object and return a view name for further processing.

Overall, Spring's @ModelAttribute annotation makes it easy to handle form submissions and bind form data to a model object. This can simplify the code and make it easier to work with form submissions in a Spring application.

2.16   Explain the use of the @Autowired annotation in Spring.

The '@Autowired' annotation in the Spring Framework is used to automatically wire beans or components together with their required dependencies. It marks a constructor, method, or field in a class to be autowired with a Spring bean, eliminating the need for XML configuration files or manual dependency injection implementations.

When '@Autowired' is used in a constructor, Spring automatically injects a suitable bean instance as a constructor argument, resolving the dependency by type. For example:

```
@Service
public class MyService {

    private final MyRepository myRepository;

    @Autowired
    public MyService(MyRepository myRepository) {
        this.myRepository = myRepository;
    }

    // ...
}
```

In this example, the '@Autowired' annotation is used on the constructor of the 'MyService' class to inject an instance of 'MyRepository'. Spring will automatically find a suitable bean of type 'MyRepository' and pass it as a constructor argument.

If two beans of the same type are available, Spring will look for a primary bean or a bean with a specific name using the '@Qualifier' annotation. For example:

```
@Service
public class MyService {

    private final MyRepository primaryRepository;
    private final MyRepository secondaryRepository;

    @Autowired
    public MyService(@Qualifier("primaryMyRepository") MyRepository
        primaryRepository,
                    @Qualifier("secondaryMyRepository") MyRepository
                        secondaryRepository) {
        this.primaryRepository = primaryRepository;
        this.secondaryRepository = secondaryRepository;
    }

    // ...
}
```

In this case, two beans of type 'MyRepository' are available, but Spring will look for beans named "primaryMyRepository" and "secondaryMyRepository" using the '@Qualifier' annotation.

'@Autowired' can also be used on a field or a method:

```
@Service
public class MyService {

    @Autowired
    private MyRepository myRepository;

    // ...

    @Autowired
    public void setMyRepository(MyRepository myRepository) {
        this.myRepository = myRepository;
    }

    // ...
}
```

Both of these approaches will inject an instance of 'MyRepository' into the 'MyService' bean, but constructor injection is generally recommended for better readability and immutable dependencies.

The '@Autowired' annotation can also be used together with other annotations, such as '@Transactional' or '@Value', to specify additional behavior for the dependency injection.

In summary, the '@Autowired' annotation in the Spring Framework is a powerful tool for easily managing dependencies between beans and components, allowing for better decoupling and simplified configuration.

2.17   What is the difference between @Component, @Service, @Repository, and @Controller annotations in Spring?

All the four annotations (@Component, @Service, @Repository, @Controller) are used for component scanning in Spring and help Spring to identify specific types of classes.

@Component is a generic annotation used for any Spring-managed component. It means that any class can be marked as a component using this annotation. For example:

```
@Component
public class MyComponent {
    // class implementation
}
```

@Service is used to annotate classes representing a service in a business logic layer. It indicates that this class is a business service and helps in implementing the Service layer. For example:

```
@Service
public class UserService {
    // class implementation
}
```

@Repository is used to annotate classes accessing the database. It automatically handles the DAO (Data Access Object) exceptions and makes it easier to implement the data access layer. For example:

```
@Repository
public class UserDaoImpl implements UserDao {
    // class implementation
}
```

@Controller is used to annotate web request handler classes. It indicates that the class is responsible for handling requests and serves as the middleman between the Model and the View. For example:

```
@Controller
public class UserController {
    // class implementation
}
```

In summary, each of the annotations represents a different type of class and helps in identifying what the class does in your Spring application. @Component is a more generic annotation, while @Service, @Repository, and @Controller represent more specific use cases of components in a Spring application.

2.18   What is the purpose of the Spring Boot framework, and how does it simplify Spring application development?

The Spring Boot framework is an open-source and widely used framework for building enterprise-level microservices and web applications based on the Spring ecosystem. It is designed to simplify and accelerate the Spring application development process by providing a streamlined, opinionated approach to configuring and deploying Spring-based applications.

The main purpose of Spring Boot is to eliminate the boiler-plate code and tedious configuration required when setting up a Spring application from scratch. With Spring Boot, developers can quickly create production-grade applications with minimal fuss, thanks to its automated configuration and dependency management.

One key advantage of Spring Boot is its ability to automatically configure many aspects of the application, such as database connection pooling, logging, and security, based on sensible defaults and best practices. Since it comes bundled with a range of libraries and plugins, developers can begin coding right away and focus on the business logic of the application, rather than spending time on setting up and configuring the Spring framework.

Spring Boot also offers a number of other features that simplify development and enhance productivity. These include:

- Embedded Servers: Spring Boot includes an embedded Tomcat, Jetty or Undertow server which can be used to package and run the application as a standalone executable JAR file, without the need for an external application server.

- Auto-configuration: It provides auto-configuration of most of the commonly used Spring components like logging, security, caching, etc. This reduces the amount of boilerplate code developers have to write.

- Spring Actuator: This feature enables developers to monitor and manage the application in production environments. It provides endpoints for managing the application, such as measuring metrics, health checks, and configuration.

In summary, Spring Boot simplifies the Spring application development process by providing a streamlined and opinionated approach to configuration and deployment. It eliminates much of the repetitive setup work required to get a Spring application up and running and allows developers to focus on the business logic of the application.

2.19   Explain the difference between Spring Boot and Spring MVC.

Spring Boot and Spring MVC are both parts of the larger Spring Framework, but they serve different purposes.

Spring Boot is a framework that provides a pre-configured environment for creating standalone Spring-based applications. It simplifies the configuration and deployment process, making it easier and faster to create production-ready applications. Spring Boot achieves this by defaulting to sensible configuration values, providing a set of starter dependencies for common use cases, and using embedded servers to simplify deployment.

On the other hand, Spring MVC is a framework that provides a model-view-controller architecture for creating web applications in the Spring Framework. It is especially useful for building RESTful web services and web applications. Spring MVC uses a front controller pattern, which means that all requests are first processed by a central controller (DispatcherServlet) before being forwarded to the appropriate handler method.

In summary, Spring Boot provides a pre-configured environment and reduces the amount of configuration required to create a Spring-based application, while Spring MVC provides a framework for building web applications with a model-view-controller architecture. While Spring Boot can be used with Spring MVC, they are independent frameworks with different goals.

2.20 What is a Spring Boot Starter, and how does it help in project setup?

Spring Boot Starter is a set of pre-configured dependencies that aims to simplify and accelerate the process of setting up and configuring a new Spring Boot project. It consists of a collection of libraries that contain pre-packaged configuration for various aspects of the application, such as web development or database connectivity.

Starter dependencies help developers to avoid the cumbersome and time-consuming task of manually searching, downloading, and configuring each individual dependency needed for their project. Instead, they can simply include a single starter dependency that automatically pulls in all necessary dependencies and settings that are relevant to their use case.

For example, suppose you want to build a web application using Spring Boot. Instead of specifying the dependencies for Tomcat, Spring MVC, and Jackson JSON parsing libraries manually, you can simply include the "spring-boot-starter-web" dependency, which includes all these dependencies and their required configurations.

Similarly, if you want to connect to a database, you can include the "spring-boot-starter-data-jpa" dependency, which includes all the necessary libraries for setting up a JPA repository and talking to a database.

By using starters, developers can save significant amounts of time and effort and focus instead on implementing their application logic. Additionally, starter dependencies also help ensure that the necessary dependencies are compatible with each other, reducing the risk of conflicts or unexpected behavior.

Overall, Spring Boot starters provide a straightforward and convenient way of setting up a new Spring Boot project, allowing developers to focus on delivering valuable features quickly and efficiently.

Chapter 3

Intermediate

3.1 What is the role of the BeanFactory interface in Spring? How is it different from ApplicationContext?

The BeanFactory interface is the primary interface for managing objects in a Spring application. It provides the basic mechanism for retrieving bean objects by their names or aliases, and also supports various methods for managing the lifecycle of these beans. The BeanFactory defines how objects are created, configured, and coordinated in a Spring application context, providing a basic container for creating, configuring, and managing bean objects.

On the other hand, the ApplicationContext is an extended version of the BeanFactory that provides additional features, such as support for message sources, internationalization, resource loading, and event publication. It also supports AOP and transaction management, providing a more complete solution for managing a Spring application.

One of the main differences between the BeanFactory and ApplicationContext is that the ApplicationContext loads all the configured bean definitions at once, at the time the context is created. This means that it pre-instantiates all singleton beans and eagerly creates other beans as requested, thereby improving the startup time of the application. In contrast, the BeanFactory lazily loads bean instances, creating them only when requested by the application.

Another important difference is that the ApplicationContext provides more advanced support for various aspects of an application, including integration with other Spring components, dependency injection, and AOP. It also provides a more configurable and extensible environment, with support for custom configuration files, overridden properties, and application-specific context hierarchy.

In summary, while the BeanFactory provides a basic container for managing bean objects, the ApplicationContext provides more advanced features for configuring and coordinating an entire Spring application. The ApplicationContext is generally the recommended choice for larger, more complex applications, while the BeanFactory may be sufficient for smaller or simpler applications.

3.2   Explain the different scopes of a Spring Bean.

In Spring, the scope of a bean defines the lifecycle of that bean object, and how many instance(s) of that object should be created by the container.

There are five standard bean scopes supported in Spring Framework:

1. Singleton: This is the default scope of a Spring Bean. When a bean is configured as a singleton, only one instance of the bean is created by the container and the same instance is returned to every request for that particular bean. If a singleton bean depends on other prototype beans, then new prototype instances will be created for each request.

2. Prototype: This scope defines that each time a bean is requested, a new instance of that bean is created. Prototype scoped beans are not cached by the container and a new instance is created each time it is requested.

3. Request: This scope of a bean is in request scope if it is to be instantiated once per HTTP request. This means that for each HTTP request, a new instance of the bean is created and maintained. This scope is typically used for web applications using Spring MVC.

4. Session: This scope of a bean is in session scope if it is to be instantiated once per HTTP session. This means that for each HTTP session, a new instance of the bean is created and maintained. This scope is typically used for web applications using Spring MVC, especially for handling user session-specific

data.

5. Global Session: This scope of a bean is in global session
scope if it is to be instantiated once per global HTTP session.
This means that for each global HTTP session (used in a portlet
context), a new instance of the bean is created and maintained.
This scope is specific to portlet-based web applications using
Spring.

There are also custom bean scopes that can be defined and
used by developers as per their specific requirements. For example, the Spring Cloud Context may define additional scopes
for beans that are specific to cloud-based deployments.

3.3   How can you create a custom scope for a Spring Bean?

In Spring, a scope defines the lifecycle of a bean and determines how long the bean will stay in the memory. Along with
the standard scopes provided by Spring, it is possible to create
custom scopes. Custom scopes allow you to define your own
lifecycle for a bean.

To create a custom scope for a Spring bean, you need to implement the 'Scope' interface. The 'Scope' interface has two
methods that need to be implemented:

1. 'String getConversationId()': This method should return a
unique identifier for the current conversation.

2. 'Object get(String name, ObjectFactory<?> objectFactory)':
This method should return the object for the given name. If

the object doesn't exist, it should be created using the 'Object-Factory' parameter and stored in the scope.

Here's an example of implementing the Scope interface to create a custom scope:

```java
public class CustomScope implements Scope {

    private ConcurrentHashMap<String, Object> scope = new
        ConcurrentHashMap<>();

    @Override
    public Object get(String name, ObjectFactory<?> objectFactory) {
        if(!scope.contains(name)) {
            // Create a new instance if it doesn't exist
            scope.put(name, objectFactory.getObject());
        }
        return scope.get(name);
    }

    @Override
    public Object remove(String name) {
        return scope.remove(name);
    }

    @Override
    public void registerDestructionCallback(String name, Runnable
        callback) {
        // register callback if needed
    }

    @Override
    public String getConversationId() {
        return UUID.randomUUID().toString();
    }

}
```

In this example, we create a custom scope using the 'ConcurrentHashMap'. In the 'get()' method, we check if the object exists in the scope. If it doesn't, we create and store a new instance using the 'ObjectFactory' parameter. The 'remove()' method removes the object from the scope, while 'registerDestructionCallback()' registers a callback to destroy the object.

Once you have implemented the 'Scope' interface, you need to register the custom scope with the 'ConfigurableBeanFactory'.

Here's an example of how to do this:

```
@Configuration
public class CustomScopeConfig {

    @Bean
    public CustomScope myCustomScope() {
        return new CustomScope();
    }

    @Autowired
    private CustomScope myCustomScope;

    @PostConstruct
    public void registerMyCustomScope() {
        ConfigurableBeanFactory beanFactory = (ConfigurableBeanFactory
            ) context.getAutowireCapableBeanFactory();
        beanFactory.registerScope("myScope", myCustomScope);
    }
}
```

In this example, we create a configuration class that registers
our custom scope with the 'ConfigurableBeanFactory'. We create an instance of our custom scope and register it with the
bean factory using the 'registerScope()' method. Now, we can
use '"myScope"' as the scope of our beans when we define them.
For example:

```
@Bean
@Scope("myScope")
public MyCustomBean myCustomBean() {
    return new MyCustomBean();
}
```

In this example, we have created a bean with the scope '"myScope"'.
This makes Spring use our custom scope to determine the lifecycle of this bean.

3.4 What is the purpose of the init-method and destroy-method attributes in Spring Bean configuration?

The 'init-method' and 'destroy-method' attributes in Spring Bean configuration are used for specifying the methods that should be called when a bean is initialized or destroyed respectively.

The 'init-method' attribute is used to specify the name of the method that should be called when a bean is initialized. This method is typically used to perform any initialization logic or setup that is required for the bean. The method should have a void return type and no arguments. Here's an example of how to specify an 'init-method' in Spring XML configuration:

```
<bean id="myBean" class="com.example.MyBean" init-method="init"/>
```

In the above example, the method 'init()' of the 'MyBean' class will be called when the 'myBean' bean is initialized.

The 'destroy-method' attribute is used to specify the name of the method that should be called when a bean is destroyed. This method is typically used to perform any cleanup logic or teardown that is required for the bean. The method should have a void return type and no arguments. Here's an example of how to specify a 'destroy-method' in Spring XML configuration:

```
<bean id="myBean" class="com.example.MyBean" destroy-method="cleanup
    "/>
```

In the above example, the method 'cleanup()' of the 'MyBean' class will be called when the 'myBean' bean is destroyed.

It's important to note that the 'init-method' and 'destroy-method' attributes are optional, and not all beans will require them. Additionally, these methods can be defined in the bean class itself instead of being specified in the XML configuration. If a bean defines both an 'init()' and '@PostConstruct' method, Spring will call both methods during initialization, but only one 'destroy()' or '@PreDestroy' method during destruction.

3.5   Explain the use of BeanPostProcessor and how it works in the Spring container.

In the Spring Framework, a BeanPostProcessor is an interface that allows Spring bean instances to be modified or enhanced before they are fully initialized. It provides two methods 'postProcessBeforeInitialization(Object bean, String beanName)' and 'postProcessAfterInitialization(Object bean, String beanName)' that are invoked for every bean in the Spring context. These methods give an opportunity to modify the bean instance before and after initialization respectively.

For example, suppose you want to log some information about every bean that is created in the Spring container. You can write an implementation of the BeanPostProcessor interface as follows:

```
import org.springframework.beans.factory.config.BeanPostProcessor;

public class LoggingBeanPostProcessor implements BeanPostProcessor {

    public Object postProcessBeforeInitialization(Object bean, String
        beanName) {
        System.out.println("Creating bean '" + beanName + "' : " + bean
            .getClass().getSimpleName());
        return bean;
```

```
    }

    public Object postProcessAfterInitialization(Object bean, String
        beanName) {
      return bean;
    }
  }
```

In this implementation, the 'postProcessBeforeInitialization()'
method logs information about the bean being created, such as
the bean name and class name. The 'postProcessAfterInitial-
ization()' method does nothing, except to return the same bean
instance.

To use this bean post-processor in a Spring application, you
need to register it with the Spring container. This can be done
either using XML configuration or Java configuration.

Using XML configuration:

```
<bean class="com.example.LoggingBeanPostProcessor"/>
```

Using Java configuration:

```
@Configuration
public class AppConfig {

  @Bean
  public LoggingBeanPostProcessor loggingBeanPostProcessor() {
    return new LoggingBeanPostProcessor();
  }
}
```

Once the bean post-processor is registered in the context, it
will be invoked for every bean creation. This allows you to
modify beans in a variety of ways. For example, you might
use BeanPostProcessor to inject additional dependencies, set
default property values or even proxy the beans for AOP.

3.6   What is the difference between constructor-based and setter-based dependency injection in Spring?

Spring supports two flavors of Dependency Injection(DI) - Constructor Injection and Setter Injection. Both approaches essentially achieve the same goal, which is to inject dependencies to a class, but they differ in how the beans are injected.

Constructor Injection involves passing dependencies as arguments to the class constructor, while Setter Injection involves exposing the class properties and providing a setter method to set the properties.

Let's discuss both approaches in detail.

Constructor-Based Injection:

Constructor-based injection is done by passing dependencies via class constructor arguments. By making use of constructor injection, we can ensure that all required dependencies are available during object instantiation. It helps in establishing a "tighter coupling" between dependent and dependency classes, thereby allowing for better compile-time checking.

```
public class Employee {
    private Address address;

    public Employee(Address address){
        this.address = address;
    }
    // ...
}
```

Note: This is just an example of how we can use Constructor injection; thereby creating an instance of a class and passing the dependency through the constructor method.

The address of an 'Employee' is injected while creating the instance of the 'Employee'. The dependency is satisfied by 'ApplicationContext' during initialization of the 'Employee' class. This approach can be useful in situations where only a single instance of a given class is needed, and where dependencies should be immutable once they have been assigned.

Constructor-based injection is generally preferred as it ensures that the object is in a valid state upon instantiation. Additionally, constructor-based injection also allows us to provide dependencies as read-only properties.

Setter-Based Injection:

Setter-based injection is done by exposing class properties and providing a corresponding setter method to set the properties. Setters enable the bean properties to be accessed after initialization by the 'Spring IoC container.'

```
public class Employee {
  private Address address;

  public void setAddress(Address address){
      this.address = address;
  }
  // ...
}
```

The above example shows how we can use Setter injection to set the 'Address' of an 'Employee'. The setter method can be used to inject the dependency separately after the instance of the 'Employee' is created.

Setter injection allows for more flexibility than constructor-based injection, as it allows us to have dependencies that can be

modified after an instance of the bean is created. This approach
is typically used when objects have optional dependencies, on
which the objects can work without. It is also used in cases
where there is a need to provide default or initial state for bean
properties.

To summarize, Constructor-based injection is preferred due to
compile time checking and in-built immutability constraints of
constructor parameters, while Setter-based injection is more
flexible, allowing for greater modification of dependencies after instantiation. Both have their place in our application, and
the choice heavily depends on our use-case or preference.

3.7   Explain the use of the @Qualifier an-
notation in Spring.

The '@Qualifier' annotation is used in Spring to distinguish between different instances of a bean type when there are multiple
candidates available for autowiring by type.

Consider a scenario where we have multiple implementation
classes of an interface, and we want to specify which one should
be injected in a particular bean. In such cases, we can annotate the implementation classes with the '@Qualifier' annotation and provide a unique value to each one. We can then use
this value in conjunction with the '@Autowired' annotation to
specify which implementation should be used for injection.

For example, lets say we have an interface called 'PaymentSer-
vice' and two implementation classes 'PaypalPaymentService'
and 'StripePaymentService'. We can annotate these implementation classes with the '@Qualifier' annotation like this:

```
@Component
@Qualifier("paypal")
public class PaypalPaymentService implements PaymentService { ... }

@Component
@Qualifier("stripe")
public class StripePaymentService implements PaymentService { ... }
```

Now we can specify which implementation to use for injection as follows:

```
@Autowired
@Qualifier("paypal")
private PaymentService paymentService;
```

Here, we have used the '@Qualifier' annotation along with '@Autowired' to tell Spring to inject an instance of 'PaypalPaymentService'.

It's important to note that '@Qualifier' annotations can be used in combination with '@Autowired' for both constructor and property-based dependency injection.

In summary, the '@Qualifier' annotation is a way to differentiate between multiple implementations of a bean type when using autowiring in Spring.

3.8   What is Spring Data Access, and how does it simplify working with databases?

Spring Data Access is a module of the Spring Framework that provides a simplified way to interact with data sources such as databases. It simplifies the database access layer by abstracting low-level details and providing a consistent API to work with different data sources.

Spring Data Access helps in the following ways:

1. Provides a JDBC abstraction layer: Spring provides a JDBC Template that simplifies database access by abstracting away low-level details such as opening and closing connections, handling transactions, and resource management. The JDBC Template provides a consistent API for working with different databases and removes the need for boilerplate code in every database operation.

2. Provides an ORM Integration layer: Spring provides integration with popular ORM (Object-Relational Mapping) frameworks like Hibernate, JPA (Java Persistence API), and MyBatis. With these integrations, you can use the ORM framework of your choice and expose the database operations through Spring's consistent API.

3. Simplifies Transaction Management: Transactions are an essential part of database operations. Spring provides a unified programming model for transaction management using annotations, eliminating the need for boilerplate code to manage transactions.

4. Provides support for NoSQL databases: Spring Data Access offers support for NoSQL databases, including MongoDB, Cassandra, and Redis. Spring provides a unified API for working with these databases, making it easier to switch between databases and maintain consistency in the application code.

5. Spring Boot Integration: Spring Boot, a popular Spring framework, provides auto-configuration for data access. This feature allows developers to configure the Spring Data Access library automatically, making development faster and more comfortable, with less boilerplate code.

In conclusion, Spring Data Access simplifies working with databases by providing a unified programming model, abstraction layers, and integration with popular databases and data sources. It reduces code complexity, increases productivity, and makes the application more maintainable.

3.9 How does the Spring Framework use JdbcTemplate for database operations?

The Spring Framework provides a template-based approach for performing database operations using JDBC's (Java Database Connectivity) template classes. One of these template classes is JdbcTemplate, which is a powerful and widely-used template class for performing various database-related operations in a Spring application.

Under the hood, JdbcTemplate delegates database operations to JDBC's core API, providing a simpler and more elegant way to work with database transactions, queries, and updates. Here are some of the key features of JdbcTemplate:

1. Data Sources - JdbcTemplate needs a Data Source object to connect to the database. Spring provides abstraction for configuring Data Sources through the DriverManagerDataSource or JndiDataSourceLookup.

2. Querying Results - JdbcTemplate simplifies the process of querying data from a database. It provides a set of query methods for executing SQL statements and returns results in the form of Java Objects. Example:

```
List<Product> products = jdbcTemplate.query("SELECT * FROM products"
  ,
```

```
new Object[]{},
new BeanPropertyRowMapper(Product.class));
```

The above code executes a SELECT statement to retrieve all the data from the 'products' table and returns the results in the form of a List of Product objects.

3. Data modification - JdbcTemplate also provides a set of methods for inserting, updating, and deleting data from a database. These methods also ensure transaction management by bundling these operations within a single transaction.

```
jdbcTemplate.update("INSERT INTO products(name, price) VALUES(?, ?)"
    ,
  new Object[]{"Product A", 150.0});
```

The above code inserts a new record into the 'products' table with name as "Product A" and price as 150.0.

4. Exception Handling - JdbcTemplate also handles all database exceptions and translates them into meaningful exceptions defined in the Spring API. This simplifies the error handling process in the application.

In summary, JdbcTemplate is a powerful and easy-to-use database access tool provided by the Spring Framework. It simplifies database access and helps to manage transactions, SQL queries, and data modifications.

3.10 Explain the concept of a Spring Transaction and the role of the Platform-TransactionManager.

A Spring Transaction is a process of managing the consistency and integrity of data during a database operation, which could be an insert, update, or delete, as it is being executed. In other words, Spring Transactions are a way of ensuring that database operations occur as a whole or not at all, known as the ACID principle (Atomicity, Consistency, Isolation, and Durability).

Spring Transactions can be managed in two ways: programmatic and declarative. Programmatic transactions are when transactions are managed by the developer within the code using Spring's TransactionTemplate or TransactionCallback interfaces. Declarative transactions, on the other hand, use metadata, such as annotations, to define the transactional aspects of a method or class.

The PlatformTransactionManager is an interface in the Spring Framework that provides an abstraction layer between the developer and the underlying transaction management system. It acts as a central source of control for transactional operations in Spring Applications. The PlatformTransactionManager interface defines a set of methods that are used to manage transactions within the application, such as beginning, committing, and rolling back transactions.

The PlatformTransactionManager interface has many implementations, including HibernateTransactionManager, JpaTransactionManager, and DataSourceTransactionManager, to name a few. Which implementation to use depends on the transaction management system used by the application.

For example, if the application is using Hibernate as the ORM framework, then the HibernateTransactionManager can be used to manage transactions. If the application is using JPA, then the JpaTransactionManager can be used. If plain JDBC is being used, then DataSourceTransactionManager can be used.

In summary, Spring Transactions are a way of ensuring consistency and integrity of data during a database operation, and the PlatformTransactionManager acts as an interface between the developer and the underlying transaction management system by providing a set of methods to manage transactions.

3.11   What is propagation behavior in Spring transaction management? List different propagation behaviors.

Propagation behavior is a feature of Spring transaction management that determines how a transaction should propagate from one method to another method in the same or different transactional context. It specifies the behavior of a transactional method when it executes in the context of an existing transaction.

Spring supports 7 different propagation behaviors:

1. REQUIRED propagation: This is the default behavior in Spring, which means that the transaction must be started in the calling method. If an existing transaction is available, it will be used. Otherwise, a new transaction will be created. This behavior ensures that a transaction is created for each method call that requires it.

2. REQUIRES_NEW propagation: This behavior always creates a new transaction, regardless of whether an existing transaction is already available or not. If an existing transaction is present, it will be suspended until the new transaction completes its execution. After that, the old transaction will be resumed.

3. SUPPORTS propagation: With this behavior, the method is executed within a transaction if one is already present. Otherwise, the method is executed without a transaction. In other words, if the calling method has an active transaction, it will be used. Otherwise, the method will be executed without a transaction.

4. MANDATORY propagation: This behavior mandates that an active transaction must already be present when the method is called. If an active transaction is not available, an exception is thrown.

5. NOT_SUPPORTED propagation: With this behavior, the method is executed without a transaction. If an active transaction is present, it will be suspended until the method completes its execution.

6. NEVER propagation: This behavior mandates that a transaction must not be present when the method is called. If an active transaction is already available, an exception is thrown.

7. NESTED propagation: This behavior creates a nested transaction, which can be rolled back or committed independently of the outer transaction. If an existing transaction is present, the method can be executed within the context of that transaction. Otherwise, a new transaction will be created. If the outer transaction is rolled back, the nested transaction will also be

rolled back. If the nested transaction is rolled back, the outer transaction can still continue.

Here's an example of the REQUIRED propagation behavior:

```
@Transactional(propagation = Propagation.REQUIRED)
public void updateCustomer(Customer customer) {
    // perform some database operations
}
```

In this example, the method updateCustomer is annotated with @Transactional and its propagation behavior is set to REQUIRED. This means that if an existing transaction is not already available, a new transaction will be created for this method to perform its operations. If a transaction is already available, it will use the existing transaction.

3.12 Explain the difference between checked and unchecked exceptions in Spring transaction management.

Checked and unchecked exceptions in Spring transaction management relate to how transactions are handled when an exception occurs.

Checked exceptions are exceptions that must be declared in the method signature or handled using a try-catch block. These exceptions are checked by the compiler at compile-time, and include exceptions like IOException and SQLException. When a checked exception occurs in a transactional method, the transaction must be rolled back by default (unless the exception is explicitly not marked as rollback-able).

On the other hand, unchecked exceptions are exceptions that do not need to be declared in the method signature or handled using a try-catch block. These exceptions are not checked by the compiler at compile-time, and include exceptions like NullPointerException and ArrayIndexOutOfBoundsException. When an unchecked exception occurs in a transactional method, the transaction is rolled back by default.

Spring transaction management provides features that allow you to customize how transactions are handled in the event of an exception, including options like marking certain exceptions as non-rollback-able or specifying a rollback policy for specific exceptions.

Here is an example of how checked and unchecked exceptions might be handled differently in a Spring transactional method:

```
@Transactional
public void updateUser(User user) throws SQLException {
    // Update user in database here
    // If there is a SQLException, the transaction will be rolled
        back by default
}


@Transactional
public void doSomething() {
    String str = null;
    // This will cause a NullPointerException, which will be treated
        as an unchecked exception
    // The transaction will be rolled back by default
    System.out.println(str.length());
}
```

3.13 What is the role of ViewResolver in Spring MVC?

In the Spring MVC framework, the ViewResolver is responsible for resolving the view names returned by the controller and returning the corresponding view object.

The ViewResolver serves as an interface between the controller and the view. When the controller's job is done, it returns the name of the view that should be used to render the output. The ViewResolver is then responsible for determining the actual view implementation to use based on the view name.

The ViewResolver interface requires implementing two methods:

1. 'resolveViewName(String viewName, Locale locale)' - This method is responsible for resolving the view name to an actual view implementation. The implementation returned by this method depends on the type of ViewResolver being used, for example, InternalResourceViewResolver or FreeMarkerViewResolver.

2. 'setViewNames(String... viewNames)' - This method is used to set the list of view names supported by the view resolver.

The ViewResolver can be configured in the Spring application context through either Java configuration or XML configuration. Spring provides several built-in ViewResolver implementations, such as InternalResourceViewResolver, which resolves JSP views, and FreeMarkerViewResolver, which resolves FreeMarker templates.

Here is an example of how to configure ViewResolver in Spring
MVC using Java configuration:

```
@Configuration
@EnableWebMvc
public class AppConfig implements WebMvcConfigurer {

    @Bean
    public ViewResolver viewResolver() {
        InternalResourceViewResolver resolver = new
            InternalResourceViewResolver();
        resolver.setPrefix("/WEB-INF/views/");
        resolver.setSuffix(".jsp");
        return resolver;
    }

    // Other configuration methods...
}
```

In this example, the InternalResourceViewResolver is used to
resolve JSP views. The 'prefix' property indicates the path to
the JSP files, and the 'suffix' property indicates the file exten-
sion. So, when the controller returns the view name "example",
the InternalResourceViewResolver will search for a JSP file with
the path "/WEB-INF/views/example.jsp".

In summary, the ViewResolver plays a crucial role in the Spring
MVC framework as it connects the controller and the view and
determines the actual view implementation based on the view
name.

3.14   Explain the use of HandlerMapping and HandlerAdapter in Spring MVC.

In Spring MVC, 'HandlerMapping' and 'HandlerAdapter' are
essential components that work together to handle incoming
requests and invoke the appropriate controller method for pro-

cessing.

'HandlerMapping' is responsible for identifying the appropriate controller method to handle an incoming request. There
are several implementations of 'HandlerMapping', each with a
different strategy for mapping requests to controller methods.
Some common implementations include:

- 'RequestMappingHandlerMapping': This implementation maps
requests based on '@RequestMapping' annotations on controller
methods. - 'BeanNameUrlHandlerMapping': This implementation maps requests based on the URL path using the names of
the controller beans.

'HandlerAdapter' is responsible for invoking the appropriate
controller method identified by the 'HandlerMapping' and preparing the output for the view layer. There are several implementations of 'HandlerAdapter', each designed to support different
types of controller methods. Some common implementations
include:

- 'RequestMappingHandlerAdapter': This implementation supports methods annotated with '@RequestMapping'. It handles
resolving method arguments and preparing the response. -
'SimpleControllerHandlerAdapter': This implementation supports controllers implementing the 'Controller' interface. It
simply invokes the 'handleRequest' method on the controller.

Together, 'HandlerMapping' and 'HandlerAdapter' make up the
controller layer of a Spring MVC application. They work together to process incoming requests, invoke the appropriate controller method, and prepare the response for the view layer.

For example, let's consider we have a Spring MVC application that has a controller named 'UserController' with a method 'getUserDetails()' that receives a request from URL "/users/1". The 'BeanNameUrlHandlerMapping' implementation of 'HandlerMapping' can find the appropriate controller bean, and the 'RequestMappingHandlerAdapter' implementation of 'HandlerAdapter' can invoke the 'getUserDetails()' method and prepare the response.

3.15 How can you implement internationalization in a Spring MVC application?

Internationalization, also known as i18n, is the process of designing and developing applications that can be easily translated into multiple languages without requiring code changes. The Spring Framework provides built-in support for i18n through its MessageSource interface. In a Spring MVC application, you can implement i18n by following these steps:

1. Declare MessageSource bean in configuration file:

```
@Configuration
public class AppConfig {

  @Bean
  public MessageSource messageSource() {
    ResourceBundleMessageSource messageSource = new
        ResourceBundleMessageSource();
    messageSource.setBasename("messages");
    return messageSource;
  }
}
```

2. Create messages_XX.properties files where XX represents the locale for each language you want to support. For ex-

ample, if you want to support English and French, you would create messages_en.properties and messages_fr.properties files. These files should be placed in the root of the classpath.

Example messages_en.properties file:

```
greeting = Hello!
farewell = Goodbye!
```

Example messages_fr.properties file:

```
greeting = Bonjour!
farewell = Au revoir!
```

3. Use MessageSource in your Spring MVC Controllers to get the translated messages:

```
@Controller
public class MyController {

    @Autowired
    private MessageSource messageSource;

    @RequestMapping("/hello")
    public ModelAndView hello(Locale locale) {
        String greeting = messageSource.getMessage("greeting", null,
            locale);
        return new ModelAndView("hello", "greeting", greeting);
    }

    @RequestMapping("/goodbye")
    public ModelAndView goodbye(Locale locale) {
        String farewell = messageSource.getMessage("farewell", null,
            locale);
        return new ModelAndView("goodbye", "farewell", farewell);
    }
}
```

In the above example, the MessageSource is injected into the controller using the @Autowired annotation. The getMessage() method is used to retrieve the translated messages for the given locale. The first argument is the key of the message in the properties file, the second is an array of objects that can be used to replace placeholders in the message, and the third is the locale.

4. Use Spring's view resolver to resolve views based on the locale:

```
@Configuration
@EnableWebMvc
public class WebMvcConfig implements WebMvcConfigurer {

    @Autowired
    private MessageSource messageSource;

    @Override
    public void configureViewResolvers(ViewResolverRegistry registry)
        {
      ResourceBundleViewResolver viewResolver = new
          ResourceBundleViewResolver();
      viewResolver.setBasename("views");
      viewResolver.setViewClass(JstlView.class);
      viewResolver.setOrder(1);
      viewResolver.setExposeContextBeansAsAttributes(true);
      viewResolver.setMessageSource(messageSource);
      registry.viewResolver(viewResolver);
    }
}
```

In this example, the ResourceBundleViewResolver is used to resolve views based on the locale. The views are defined in messages_XX.properties files located in the root of the classpath. The view resolver sets the order to 1 to ensure that it is used before other view resolvers. The setExposeContextBeansAsAttributes method is used to make the MessageSource bean available in the JSP page using the $messageSource attribute.

5. Use Spring's <spring:message> tag in JSP pages to display translated messages:

```
<%@taglib uri="http://www.springframework.org/tags" prefix="spring"
    %>

<html>
  <head>
    <title><spring:message code="title" /></title>
  </head>
```

```
<body>
  <h1><spring:message code="greeting" /></h1>
  <p><spring:message code="intro" /></p>
  <a href="<c:url␣value="/goodbye"␣/>"><spring:message code="link
      " /></a>
</body>
</html>
```

In the above example, the <spring:message> tag is used to retrieve the translated messages from the MessageSource bean.
The code attribute specifies the key of the message in the properties file. The <c:url> tag is used to add context path to link.

These are the steps to implement internationalization in a Spring
MVC application. By following these steps, your application
will be able to support multiple languages seamlessly.

3.16 What is Spring Security, and how does it integrate with Spring MVC?

Spring Security is a powerful and highly customizable security
framework for Java applications, built on top of the Spring
Framework. As the name suggests, Spring Security is designed
to provide authentication and authorization services to secure
your application against unauthorized access and attacks.

Spring Security can be integrated with Spring MVC (Model-
View-Controller) to provide secure access to resources and services of an application. One way to integrate Spring Security with Spring MVC is by configuring a security filter chain
that intercepts incoming requests based on the specified security rules and policies.

Here's an overview of the steps involved in integrating Spring

Security with Spring MVC:

1. Configure Spring Security: This involves defining a security config class that extends WebSecurityConfigurerAdapter, and overriding the configure(HttpSecurity http) method to specify the security rules and policies for your application.

For example, you can configure authentication (i.e., how users are authenticated), access control (i.e., who can access which resources), and CSRF protection (to defend against cross-site request forgery attacks).

2. Configure Spring MVC: Next, you need to configure Spring MVC to work with Spring Security. This involves adding a DelegatingFilterProxy to your web application context, which acts as a filter to intercept incoming requests and pass them to the Spring Security filter chain.

The DelegatingFilterProxy delegates requests to the Spring Security filter chain to apply authentication and authorization rules to the request.

3. Secure your URLs: You can secure your application URLs using Spring Security by configuring URL-based access control. This involves specifying the roles that are allowed to access each URL.

For example, you can configure '/admin/**' URLs to require authentication and authorization by users with the 'ADMIN' role.

4. Use Security annotations: Spring Security also provides annotations that can be used to secure specific methods or operations within your application.

For example, you can annotate a method with @PreAuthorize("hasRole('ROLE_ADMIN')") to restrict its access to users with the 'ADMIN' role.

In summary, Spring Security provides powerful security features that can be easily integrated with Spring MVC to secure your application against unauthorized access and attacks. By configuring a security filter chain and using Spring Security annotations, you can specify the authentication and authorization rules and policies for your application.

3.17   Explain how Spring Boot's auto-configuration feature works.

Spring Boot's auto-configuration feature analyzes the classpath and automatically configures necessary components based on the dependencies it finds. This allows for a quicker and easier setup of Spring applications with less configuration needed.

When starting up a Spring Boot application, the auto-configuration component reads the metadata of the dependencies in the classpath to identify the necessary configurations for the application to run. These configurations typically include creating the appropriate beans, setting properties, and configuring other components such as Servlets, databases, message brokers, and more.

For example, if a Spring Boot application has a dependency on the Spring Data JPA library, Spring Boot will automatically configure the necessary components to connect to a database and perform database operations without much configuration. The auto-configuration feature will provide sensible defaults for the database driver, database dialect, and other database properties based on the database detected on the classpath.

The auto-configuration feature is also customizable. Developers can customize and override the default configurations by providing their own custom configuration files or overriding properties in application.properties. This allows developers to fine-tune their applications behavior and ensure that the application behaves in the expected way.

In summary, Spring Boot's auto-configuration feature makes it easier and faster to set up Spring applications by automating the configuration process based on the dependencies found in the classpath. Developers can extend and customize the auto-configuration behavior to fit their needs.

3.18 What is a Spring Boot Actuator, and how does it help in monitoring and managing applications?

Spring Boot Actuator is a powerful feature of the Spring Boot framework that provides a production-ready set of tools and endpoints to monitor and manage Spring Boot applications. It enables you to monitor various aspects of your application such as application health, metrics, logs, environment details, etc. in real-time. Additionally, it provides the capability to manage your Spring Boot application remotely by exposing endpoints for various operations.

Actuator exposes endpoints via HTTP or JMX that can be used to retrieve information or perform actions such as checking the system health, viewing thread dumps, managing log levels, and viewing environment properties, to name a few. These endpoints can be accessed using a web browser or a HTTP client like Postman or cURL.

Here are some examples of how Spring Boot Actuator helps in monitoring and managing applications:

1. Health Endpoint: The health endpoint provides information about the health of your application. It returns an HTTP response code indicating whether the application is up or down. Additionally, you can configure custom health checks to verify if your application is healthy.

2. Metrics Endpoint: The metrics endpoint provides information about the application's metrics, such as memory usage, CPU usage, HTTP requests, etc. It helps you identify performance issues in real-time and optimize the application.

3. Logging Endpoint: The logging endpoint provides the ability to view and modify log levels at runtime, without the need to restart the application. This helps in troubleshooting issues in production environments without downtime.

4. Environment Endpoint: The environment endpoint provides information about the application's properties and configuration, including system properties, environment variables, and other application properties.

Overall, Spring Boot Actuator provides a powerful set of tools and endpoints for monitoring and managing Spring Boot applications in production environments. It helps developers and DevOps teams quickly diagnose and fix issues, improve performance, and optimize the application for better reliability and scalability.

3.19 Explain Spring Boot Profiles, and how they can be used to manage application configurations.

Spring Boot Profiles are a powerful feature that allows developers to define different sets of configuration options for a single application, depending on the environment it is running in. This means that specific properties or settings can be specified for different stages of development, testing, and production.

Profiles can be defined in a variety of ways, but typically they are simply a predefined set of properties that can be included or excluded depending on which profile is active. For example, a development profile might have a certain set of properties enabled, while production might have a different set of properties enabled.

Spring Boot Profiles are defined in several ways:

1. Using application.properties or application.yml files. Developers can create different configuration files for different profiles, and Spring Boot will automatically load the appropriate file depending on the active profile.

For example, if the active profile is "development", Spring Boot will load the configuration properties from "application-development .properties" or "application-development.yml" files in the application classpath.

2. Using the "spring.profiles.active" system property, environment variable or command-line argument. Developers can specify which profiles should be active when running the application, by setting the "spring.profiles.active" system property, environ-

ment variable or command-line argument.

For example, if we want to activate the "development" profile
when running the application with command-line argument, we
can use this command:

```
java -jar myapp.jar --spring.profiles.active=development
```

3. Programmatically, using the Spring Environment API. Developers can also programmatically set an active profile using
the environment API.

For example, to activate the "test" profile programmatically,
we can use this code:

```
ConfigurableEnvironment env = context.getEnvironment();
env.setActiveProfiles("test");
```

Profiles are particularly useful for managing application configurations in different environments. For example, we might
want to have different database configurations for production
and development environments. By defining a profile for each
environment, we can easily specify the appropriate configuration file or properties for each environment, without having to
manually configure each individual component.

Here is an example of how to use profiles with database configuration:

```
@Configuration
@Profile("development")
public class DevelopmentDatabaseConfig {

    @Bean
    public DataSource dataSource() {
        // Development database configuration
    }
}

@Configuration
```

```
@Profile("production")
public class ProductionDatabaseConfig {

    @Bean
    public DataSource dataSource() {
        // Production database configuration
    }
}
```

In the above example, we define two different database configurations for the "development" and "production" profiles. The appropriate configuration will be automatically loaded based on the active profile.

In conclusion, Spring Boot Profiles are a powerful and flexible way to manage application configurations. By defining different profiles for different environments, developers can easily switch between configurations and customize application behavior based on runtime environment.

3.20 What are the differences between Spring Boot's embedded servlet containers (Tomcat, Jetty, and Undertow)?

Spring Boot provides support for several embedded servlet containers including Tomcat, Jetty, and Undertow. These containers are built into the application, which means that you can run your application as a standalone executable without needing to install and configure a separate application server.

Here are some of the key differences between these containers:

1. Tomcat is the most widely used servlet container in the

world. It is known for its stability and maturity. Tomcat provides support for the Servlet and JSP specifications, as well as support for WebSocket, JMX, and JNDI. If you have an existing Tomcat-based application, Spring Boot's embedded Tomcat container is likely the best choice.

2. Jetty is another popular servlet container that is known for its speed and low memory usage. Jetty provides support for the latest Servlet and WebSocket specifications, as well as support for SPDY and HTTP/2. Jetty is particularly well-suited for high-throughput applications that require low latency.

3. Undertow is a relatively new servlet container that was developed by JBoss. It is designed for high-performance applications that require a low memory footprint. Undertow provides support for the Servlet and WebSocket specifications, as well as support for HTTP/2. Undertow is particularly well-suited for microservices-based architectures.

In terms of choosing which servlet container to use with Spring Boot, the decision ultimately depends on your specific use case. If you have an existing Tomcat-based application, Spring Boot's embedded Tomcat container is likely the best choice. If you are building a new application that requires high throughput, Jetty may be the best choice. If you are building a microservices-based architecture and require a low memory footprint, Undertow may be the best choice.

Here's an example of how to configure your Spring Boot application to use the embedded Tomcat container:

```
@SpringBootApplication
public class MyApplication {

    public static void main(String[] args) {
        SpringApplication.run(MyApplication.class, args);
    }
```

```
@Bean
public TomcatServletWebServerFactory tomcatFactory() {
   return new TomcatServletWebServerFactory() {
      @Override
      protected void postProcessContext(Context context) {
         SecurityConstraint securityConstraint = new
            SecurityConstraint();
         securityConstraint.setUserConstraint("CONFIDENTIAL");
         SecurityCollection collection = new SecurityCollection();
         collection.addPattern("/*");
         securityConstraint.addCollection(collection);
         context.addConstraint(securityConstraint);
      }
   };
}

@Bean
public ServletWebServerFactory servletContainer() {
   return new TomcatServletWebServerFactory();
}
}
```

In this example, we are configuring a TomcatServletWebServer-
Factory bean that sets up a security constraint that requires all
requests to be made over HTTPS. We are also configuring a
default ServletWebServerFactory bean that uses the Tomcat-
ServletWebServerFactory by default.

Chapter 4

Advanced

4.1 Explain the concept of Spring Bean lifecycle, and how you can intercept various lifecycle events.

The Spring Bean lifecycle refers to the various stages that a Bean goes through, from its instantiation to its destruction. Understanding the lifecycle of a Bean is important because it helps developers manage the creation and destruction of beans and the dependencies between them. Spring provides a set of callback interfaces that allow developers to intercept various lifecycle events and execute code accordingly.

There are several stages in the Spring Bean lifecycle, which can be divided into the following phases:

1. Instantiation: During this phase, the Spring container reads the bean definition and creates an instance of the object using a constructor or a

factory method.

2. Populate properties: Once the object is instantiated, Spring then populates its properties either by calling a setter method or using reflection.

3. BeanNameAware: This is the first callback interface that can be used to intercept a Bean's lifecycle. The container will call the setBeanName() method of the BeanNameAware class, which you can use to modify the name of the bean or perform any other operations related to the bean's name.

4. BeanFactoryAware: During this phase, the container will call the setBeanFactory() method of the BeanFactoryAware interface, which can be used to get a reference to the bean factory and perform any operations related to the factory.

5. Pre-initialization: This is the phase where custom initialization can be performed using the InitializingBean or @PostConstruct annotation.

6. Initialization: During this phase, the container will call any custom initialization method defined by the developer using the init-method attribute or the InitializingBean interface.

7. Post-initialization: This phase allows for any additional post-processing of the bean using the BeanPostProcessor interface.

8. Bean ready to use: The bean is now ready to be used and can be accessed by other beans or the application.

9. Shutdown: The final phase is when the bean is destroyed or shut down. This can be achieved by calling the destroy() method using the DisposableBean interface or using the destroy-method attribute in the bean definition.

To intercept these lifecycle events, Spring provides developers with various callback interfaces, including

- 'BeanNameAware': This interface allows the bean to know its name as provided by the container.

- 'BeanFactoryAware': When beans implement this interface, the container provides them with the 'BeanFactory' reference.

- 'InitializingBean': This interface provides a callback to initialize the bean after its properties have been set by the container.

- 'DisposableBean': This interface provides a callback to perform any cleanup of resources or state before the bean is destroyed by the container.

- 'BeanPostProcessor': This interface provides two callbacks 'postProcess-BeforeInitialization' and 'postProcessAfterInitialization' that allow you to intercept and change the initialization behavior of a bean.

Developers can use these interfaces to execute code at different stages of the Bean lifecycle, for example:

1. BeanNameAware

```java
public class DemoBean implements BeanNameAware {

    private String beanName;

    public void setBeanName(String beanName) {
        this.beanName = beanName;
        System.out.println("Setting beanName: " + beanName);
    }

    public String getBeanName() {
        return beanName;
    }
}
```

2. InitializingBean:

```java
public class DemoBean implements InitializingBean {

    private String name;

    public void afterPropertiesSet() {
        this.name = "Demo Bean";
        System.out.println("Bean is initialized: " + this.name);
    }

    public String getName() {
        return name;
    }
}
```

3. BeanPostProcessor:

```java
public class DemoBeanPostProcessor implements BeanPostProcessor {

    public Object postProcessBeforeInitialization(Object bean,
        String beanName) throws BeansException {
```

```
        System.out.println("Before_initialization:_" + beanName);
        return bean;
    }

    public Object postProcessAfterInitialization(Object bean, String
        beanName) throws BeansException {
        System.out.println("After_initialization:_" + beanName);
        return bean;
    }
}
```

In conclusion, understanding the Spring Bean lifecycle and how to intercept its various stages is an essential aspect of managing beans and their dependencies effectively. With the lifecycle callback interfaces provided by Spring framework, developers can perform custom operations at different stages during the bean's lifecycle, modify its behavior, or perform cleanup when the bean is no longer needed.

4.2   How can you configure a Spring Bean using Java-based configuration instead of XML-based configuration?

Spring provides two ways of defining and configuring beans, XML-based and Java-based configuration. While XML configuration is widely used, Java-based configuration has gained popularity among Spring developers due to its simplicity, type-safety, and code readability. Here are the steps to configure Spring Beans using Java-based configuration:

1. Enable Java-based configuration: To use Java-based configuration in a Spring application, you need to enable it by adding the '@Configuration' annotation to a Java class. This annotation indicates that the class contains Spring configura-

tion information.

```
@Configuration
public class AppConfig {
    // bean definitions go here
}
```

2. Define the Beans: To define a Bean in Java-based configuration, you can create a method and annotate it with '@Bean'. The method should return the bean that you want to configure.

```
@Configuration
public class AppConfig {

    @Bean
    public MyBean myBean() {
        return new MyBean();
    }
}
```

3. Customizing Bean Properties: If you need to set custom properties of a bean, you can do so by calling bean methods on the created bean instance.

```
@Configuration
public class AppConfig {

    @Bean
    public MyBean myBean() {
        MyBean bean = new MyBean();
        bean.setFoo("foo");
        bean.setBar("bar");
        return bean;
    }
}
```

4. Injecting dependencies: You can inject dependencies into a bean by specifying method parameters annotated with '@Autowired'.

```
@Configuration
public class AppConfig {

    @Bean
    public MyBean myBean(Foo foo, Bar bar) {
```

```
        return new MyBean(foo, bar);
    }
}
```

5. Importing Configuration classes: If your application has
multiple configuration classes, you can import them into a main
configuration class using the '@Import' annotation.

```
@Configuration
@Import({DataSourceConfig.class, MailConfig.class})
public class AppConfig {
    // bean definitions go here
}
```

In conclusion, Spring Framework provides a flexible and powerful configuration mechanism for creating and managing beans,
and the Java-based configuration approach provides a better
way to write the configuration in a type-safe and easy-to-understand
manner.

4.3   Explain the difference between @Bean and @Component annotations in Spring.

In the Spring Framework, both '@Bean' and '@Component'
annotations are used to declare beans, but they have different
purposes and use cases.

'@Component' is a stereotype annotation that identifies a class
as a Spring-managed component. This annotation tells Spring
to create a bean instance of the annotated class and register
it in the application context. Spring will automatically detect
and create instances of all classes annotated with '@Compo-
nent' when it scans the project's classpath. For example, the

following code snippet shows how to use '@Component' annotation to create a bean instance of a class:

```
@Component
public class MyComponent {
    // class implementation
}
```

On the other hand, the '@Bean' annotation is used to explicitly declare a bean instance in a Java configuration class. This annotation is used in conjunction with a method that produces a bean instance when invoked. The method annotated with '@Bean' creates and returns the instance of the bean, and Spring manages it in the application context. For example, the following code shows how to use '@Bean' annotation to manually create a bean instance in a configuration class:

```
@Configuration
public class MyConfig {
    @Bean
    public MyBean myBean() {
        return new MyBean();
    }
}
```

As you can see from the above code snippet, '@Bean' tells Spring that the method 'myBean()' will produce a bean instance, and Spring manages the instance in the application context.

In summary, '@Component' is used for automatic bean detection and registration, while '@Bean' is used for manual bean declaration and configuration.

4.4   What is the role of ApplicationContextAware and BeanNameAware interfaces in Spring?

The ApplicationContextAware and BeanNameAware interfaces are two callback interfaces provided by the Spring framework to allow a Spring-managed bean to interact with its container.

The ApplicationContextAware interface allows a Spring-managed bean to get a reference to the ApplicationContext instance in which it is running. Essentially, this interface provides a way to access the Spring container and its contained beans at runtime. By implementing this interface, a bean can get access to other beans managed by the container or control the container's behavior.

Here is an example of the use of the ApplicationContextAware interface:

```
import org.springframework.context.ApplicationContextAware;
import org.springframework.context.ApplicationContext;

public class MyBean implements ApplicationContextAware {

    private ApplicationContext context;

    @Override
    public void setApplicationContext(ApplicationContext context) {
        this.context = context;
    }

    //Methods that use the context object
}
```

The BeanNameAware interface provides the name of the bean in the Spring container to the bean itself. By implementing this interface, a bean can find out its name in the container.

Here is an example of the use of the BeanNameAware interface:

```
import org.springframework.beans.factory.BeanNameAware;

public class MyBean implements BeanNameAware {

    private String beanName;

    @Override
    public void setBeanName(String name) {
        this.beanName = name;
    }

    //Method that uses the beanName field
}
```

In conclusion, the ApplicationContextAware and BeanNameAware interfaces provide a way to interact with the Spring container and the beans it manages. By implementing these interfaces, a bean gains access to the container and can perform operations on it, such as getting references to other beans and controlling the container's behavior.

4.5   How can you achieve method-level security using Spring Security?

Spring Security provides different ways to achieve method-level security in our applications. Method-level security controls the access level of a specific method execution in a class. It is useful when we want to secure individual methods based on different roles and permissions.

There are two ways in which we can achieve method-level security using Spring Security:

1. Using @Secured annotation: In this approach, we need to annotate the method with the @Secured annotation and specify the role or permission required to access that method.

For example, let's say we have a UserService class that has a method saveUser() that should be only accessible to users with the "ADMIN" role. We can achieve this by adding the @Secured("ROLE_ADMIN") annotation before the method declaration:

```
@Service
public class UserService {
    @Secured("ROLE_ADMIN")
    public void saveUser(User user) {
        //Some business logic here
    }
}
```

2. Using AOP: In this approach, we define an aspect that intercepts the method execution and applies the security rules. We need to configure the aspect and define the security rules in the application context XML file. For example, let's say we have a ProductService class that has a method updateProduct() that should be only accessible to users with the "PRODUCT_MANAGER" role. We can achieve this by configuring an aspect using AOP:

```
<bean id="mySecurityAspect" class="org.springframework.security.
    access.intercept.aspectj.aspect.AnnotationSecurityAspect">
    <property name="securityInterceptor" ref="
        methodSecurityInterceptor"/>
</bean>

<bean id="methodSecurityInterceptor" class="org.springframework.
    security.access.intercept.aopalliance.
    MethodSecurityInterceptor">
    <property name="authenticationManager" ref="
        authenticationManager"/>
    <property name="accessDecisionManager" ref="
        accessDecisionManager"/>
</bean>

<bean id="accessDecisionManager" class="org.springframework.
    security.access.vote.UnanimousBased">
    <constructor-arg>
        <list>
            <bean class="org.springframework.security.access.vote.
                RoleVoter"/>
            <bean class="org.springframework.security.access.vote.
                AuthenticatedVoter"/>
        </list>
```

```
        </constructor-arg>
    </bean>

    <bean id="productService" class="com.example.service.
        ProductService"/>

    <aop:config>
        <aop:aspect id="productServiceSecurity" ref="mySecurityAspect
            ">
            <aop:pointcut expression="execution(*␣com.example.service.
                ProductService.updateProduct(..))"/>
            <aop:around method="org.springframework.security.access.
                intercept.aspectj.aspect.AnnotationSecurityAspect.
                aspectOf()"/>
        </aop:aspect>
    </aop:config>
```

In the above example, we defined an aspect that applies to
the updateProduct() method of ProductService class. We also
configured a method security interceptor to manage the access
control to this method. Finally, we defined an access decision
manager that checks whether the user has the required permission to access the method.

Overall, both approaches can be used to achieve method-level
security with Spring Security. Using the @Secured annotation
is ideal for simple and straightforward methods whereas AOP
is better suited for larger and more complex applications.

4.6   What is the difference between pro-grammatic and declarative transaction management in Spring?

In Java Spring Framework, transaction management can be
managed programmatically or declaratively.

Programmatic transaction management involves manually controlling the transaction behavior with the help of Spring's transaction manager API. This approach gives developers more control over the transaction's code flow and can facilitate cases where different transactions need to be managed in different ways. Programmatic transaction management often involves the use of try-catch-finally blocks to correctly handle transaction outcomes (i.e., committing transaction, rolling back transaction or leaving it open).

Here's an example of programmatic transaction management in Spring:

```
@Autowired
private PlatformTransactionManager transactionManager;

@Transactional
public void performFoo() {
    TransactionStatus status = transactionManager.getTransaction(new
        DefaultTransactionDefinition());
    try {
        //perform database operations
        transactionManager.commit(status);
    } catch (Exception e) {
        transactionManager.rollback(status);
    }
}
```

Declarative transaction management in Spring allows transaction management to be specified using XML or annotations, which describes the configuration of the transaction behavior. This approach offers more clarity and less clutter in the code, as the developer only needs to specify rules for transaction management instead of implementing it in code.

Here's an example of declarative transaction management in Spring using annotations:

```
@Transactional
public void performFoo() {
    //perform database operations
}
```

In this example, any method marked with the '@Transactional' annotation is wrapped in a transaction that is started just before the method is invoked and either committed or rolled back when the method ends.

In conclusion, the difference between programmatic and declarative transaction management in Spring is that programmatic transaction management involves manually controlling the transaction behavior with code, while declarative transaction management uses annotations or XML configurations to specify the rules for transaction management. Both approaches have their merits and limitations, and the choice between the two depends on the specific requirements and constraints of the project at hand.

4.7 How can you use Spring AOP for implementing cross-cutting concerns in an application?

Spring AOP (Aspect-oriented programming) is a powerful feature of the Spring framework that you can use to implement cross-cutting concerns in your application. Cross-cutting concerns refer to any functionality that needs to be applied across multiple components or layers of your application, such as logging, security, and transaction management.

To implement cross-cutting concerns using Spring AOP, you need to follow these steps:

1. Define an aspect: An aspect encapsulates the cross-cutting concern and specifies the join points where it will be applied.

Join points are points in the code where the cross-cutting concern needs to be applied, such as method executions or object
creations.

For example, let's say that you want to log the execution time
of all the methods in your application. You can define an aspect that captures the execution time of all the methods by
specifying the join point as method execution.

```
@Aspect
@Component
public class LoggingAspect {

    @Around("execution(*␣com.example.myapp..*.*(..))")
    public Object logExecutionTime(ProceedingJoinPoint joinPoint)
        throws Throwable {

        long startTime = System.currentTimeMillis();

        Object result = joinPoint.proceed();

        long timeTaken = System.currentTimeMillis() - startTime;

        System.out.println("Execution␣time␣of␣" + joinPoint.
            getSignature() + "␣=␣" + timeTaken + "␣ms");

        return result;
    }
}
```

In this example, the '@Aspect' annotation marks the class as
an aspect. The '@Component' annotation makes Spring create
a bean for this class. The '@Around' annotation captures the
method execution join point for all the methods in the 'com.ex-
ample.myapp' package and its sub-packages.

The 'logExecutionTime' method is the advice that encapsulates the cross-cutting concern, which in this case is logging
the execution time of the method. The 'ProceedingJoinPoint'
parameter specifies the join point where the advice is applied.
The 'proceed()' method invocation executes the target method
and returns its result.

2. Configure AOP: After defining the aspect, you need to configure AOP in your Spring configuration file. You can either use XML-based configuration or Java-based configuration for this.

For example, if you are using XML-based configuration, you need to define the 'aop:aspectj-autoproxy' element in your application context file:

```
<beans>
    <aop:aspectj-autoproxy />
    <bean id="loggingAspect" class="com.example.myapp.LoggingAspect"
        />
</beans>
```

If you are using Java-based configuration, you can use the '@EnableAspectJAutoProxy' annotation on your configuration class and declare the aspect as a bean:

```
@Configuration
@EnableAspectJAutoProxy
public class AppConfig {

    @Bean
    public LoggingAspect loggingAspect() {
        return new LoggingAspect();
    }
}
```

3. Apply the aspect: Finally, you need to apply the aspect to the components where the cross-cutting concern needs to be applied. This can be done by annotating the component with the aspect's pointcut expression.

For example, let's say that you want to log the execution time of the 'MyService' class. You can apply the 'LoggingAspect' aspect to this class by annotating it with '@LoggingAspect' annotation, which in turn specifies the pointcut expression for method execution:

```
@Service
```

```
@LoggingAspect
public class MyService {

    public void doSomething() {
        // ...
    }
}
```

In this example, the '@Service' annotation marks the class as a Spring service component. The '@LoggingAspect' annotation specifies that the 'LoggingAspect' aspect should be applied to this class. The pointcut expression in the 'LoggingAspect' aspect defines the join point as method execution for all the methods in the 'com.example.myapp' package and its sub-packages.

In summary, Spring AOP provides a powerful mechanism for implementing cross-cutting concerns in your application. It allows you to encapsulate the cross-cutting concern in an aspect, configure AOP in your Spring configuration file, and apply the aspect to the components where the cross-cutting concern needs to be applied.

4.8   Explain the difference between a Join-Point, a Pointcut, and an Advice in Spring AOP.

In Spring AOP, JoinPoint, Pointcut, and Advice are three key concepts that help developers to implement cross-cutting concerns in their applications.

A JoinPoint is a point during the execution of a program, such as method call, constructor call, or exception handler execution. In Spring AOP, JoinPoints are identified by the framework and become the targets of weaving.

A Pointcut is a set of one or more JoinPoints where an Advice should be applied. Pointcut helps developers to specify what types of JoinPoints should be intercepted and executed with the Advice. For example, a Pointcut can include all the methods in a specific class or all the methods annotated with a certain annotation.

An Advice is a piece of code that runs at a specific JoinPoint in a programs execution. In Spring AOP, there are several types of advice, including BeforeAdvice, AfterAdvice, and AroundAdvice. BeforeAdvice runs before the JoinPoint executed; AfterAdvice runs after the JoinPoint executed, and AroundAdvice runs before and after the JoinPoint executed, allowing developers to customize how the JoinPoint behavior accordingly.

To better understand these concepts, let's take a look at the following example:

```
@Aspect
public class LoggingAspect {

    @Pointcut("execution(* com.example.service.*.*(..))")
    public void serviceMethods() {}

    @Before("serviceMethods()")
    public void logBefore(JoinPoint joinPoint) {
        System.out.println("Before method execution: " + joinPoint.
            getSignature());
    }

    @After("serviceMethods()")
    public void logAfter(JoinPoint joinPoint) {
        System.out.println("After method execution: " + joinPoint.
            getSignature());
    }

    @Around("serviceMethods()")
    public Object logAround(ProceedingJoinPoint joinPoint) throws
        Throwable {
        System.out.println("Before method execution: " + joinPoint.
            getSignature());
```

```
Object result = joinPoint.proceed();
System.out.println("After method execution: " + joinPoint.
    getSignature());
return result;
    }
}
```

In the above code snippet, we have defined an Aspect called LoggingAspect. Within the LoggingAspect, we have defined a Pointcut 'serviceMethods()' that matches all the methods in the 'com.example.service' package.

We have also defined three Advices, Before, After, and Around, which are applied to Pointcut 'serviceMethods()'.

The Before advice logs a message before the JoinPoint is called. The After advice logs a message after the JoinPoint is completed successfully. The Around advice logs a message both before and after the JoinPoint is called, and in this case, it also intercepts the JoinPoint execution.

Overall, these three concepts are essential to implementing Aspect-Oriented Programming in Spring AOP, giving developers more control over their applications' behavior and maintainability.

4.9   What is the role of the Spring Expression Language (SpEL), and how is it used in a Spring application?

The Spring Expression Language (SpEL) is a powerful expression language that is used in the Spring Framework. Its role is to provide a flexible and powerful way to evaluate expressions, manipulate data, and access Spring beans and properties.

SpEL is used extensively in a Spring application, particularly in the configuration and runtime settings. It can be used in XML and annotation-based configurations, as well as in the code during runtime. Here are some scenarios where SpEL is used:

1. Configuring properties: SpEL is used in property placeholders to inject dynamic values into the configuration files. For example, you can use SpEL to configure properties like database URLs, email addresses, and other values that are subject to change.

```
<bean id="myBean" class="com.example.MyBean">
  <property name="url" value="#{dataSource.url}" />
</bean>
```

In this example, the URL property of the MyBean has been configured using SpEL to get the URL from a dataSource bean.

2. Conditional bean creation: SpEL can also be used to decide whether or not to create a bean based on some conditions. For example, you can use SpEL to conditionally create a bean based on the environment or some other factors.

```
<bean id="myBean" class="com.example.MyBean"
    c:arg1="${arg1}" c:arg2="${arg2}">
    <conditional-on-expression>#{systemProperties['env'] == 'prod'
        }</conditional-on-expression>
</bean>
```

In this example, the bean is created only if the system property 'env' is set to 'prod'.

3. Parameterizing annotations: Annotations are commonly used in Spring-based applications for defining various aspects of the application. SpEL can be used to parameterize annotation values at runtime.

```
@GetMapping(value = "/books/{id}")
@PreAuthorize("hasRole(#user.role)")
public Book getBookById(@PathVariable long id,
    @AuthenticationPrincipal UserDetails user) {
  // implementation
}
```

In this example, the hasRole() expression in the PreAuthorize annotation is using SpEL to get the role of the user and pass it as a parameter to the hasRole() method.

Overall, SpEL is a powerful addition to the Spring Framework that facilitates a flexible configuration and runtime settings for a Spring application.

4.10   How can you implement caching in a Spring application using Spring Cache abstraction?

Caching is an essential feature of any application that aims to improve performance and reduce external dependencies. In a Spring application, we can implement caching using the Spring Cache abstraction. The Spring Cache abstraction provides a consistent way of working with different caching technologies like EhCache, Redis, and others.

Heres a step-by-step guide on how to implement Caching in a Spring application using Spring Cache abstraction:

Step 1: Add Spring Cache Dependencies Add the Spring Boot dependencies for the caching abstraction and for the caching provider which you want to use. For example, the following dependencies can be added to the 'pom.xml' file:

```
<dependency>
    <groupId>org.springframework.boot</groupId>
    <artifactId>spring-boot-starter-cache</artifactId>
</dependency>

<dependency>
    <groupId>org.springframework.boot</groupId>
    <artifactId>spring-boot-starter-data-redis</artifactId>
</dependency>
```

Step 2: Add Cache Configuration Add a caching configuration class to the application. The configuration class must include the '@EnableCaching' annotation that enables caching support in the application. This class can also include specific configurations for the chosen caching provider.

```
@Configuration
@EnableCaching
public class CacheConfiguration {

    @Autowired
    private RedisConnectionFactory redisConnectionFactory;

    @Bean
    public RedisTemplate<String, Object> redisTemplate() {
        RedisTemplate<String, Object> redisTemplate = new
            RedisTemplate<>();
        redisTemplate.setConnectionFactory(redisConnectionFactory);
        redisTemplate.setKeySerializer(new StringRedisSerializer());
        redisTemplate.setValueSerializer(new
            GenericJackson2JsonRedisSerializer());
        return redisTemplate;
    }

    @Bean
    public CacheManager cacheManager() {
        RedisCacheManager cacheManager = RedisCacheManager.builder(
            redisConnectionFactory)
                .cacheDefaults(RedisCacheConfiguration.
                    defaultCacheConfig()
                        .entryTtl(Duration.ofMinutes(10)))
                .build();
        return cacheManager;
    }
}
```

In the above example, we create a RedisTemplate bean for Redis cache provider and define the RedisCacheManager. Redis-

CacheConfiguration is used to specify the cache expiry time.

Step 3: Use Spring Cache Abstraction Once the caching configuration setup is complete, you can start using the Spring Cache
abstraction. You can annotate methods with the '@Cacheable',
'@CachePut', and '@CacheEvict' annotations to take advantage
of caching.

The '@Cacheable' annotation indicates that a method result
is cached and retrieved from the cache if the same method is
called again with the same parameters. If the method is called
with a new parameter, the result is re-evaluated and cached.

```
@Service
public class UserService {

    @Autowired
    private UserRepository userRepository;

    @Cacheable(value = "users")
    public User getUserByEmail(String email) {
        return userRepository.findByEmail(email);
    }

}
```

In the above example, the 'getUserByEmail' method result will
be stored in a cache named 'users'.

The '@CachePut' annotation updates the cache with the resulting object of a method call. This annotation is useful when you
need to update a cache entry without waiting for it to expire.

```
@Service
public class UserService {

    @Autowired
    private UserRepository userRepository;

    @CachePut(value = "users", key = "#user.email")
    public User createUser(User user) {
        return userRepository.save(user);
    }
```

```
}
```

In the above example, the 'createUser' method creates a new user record in the database, and its result is stored in the cache named 'users'.

The '@CacheEvict' annotation removes a cache entry when a method is called. This annotation typically used when you're finalizing an operation that could leave data in the cache invalid or stale.

```
@Service
public class UserService {

    @Autowired
    private UserRepository userRepository;

    @CacheEvict(value = "users", key = "#user.email")
    public void deleteUserByEmail(User user) {
        userRepository.delete(user);
    }

}
```

In the above example, the 'deleteUserByEmail' method removes the user record from the database and its cache entry from a cache named 'users'.

Conclusion: Using Spring Cache Abstraction simplifies caching within a Spring application, providing a consistent way of working with different caching technologies. Caching can be implemented easily in a Spring application using the '@Cacheable', '@CachePut', and '@CacheEvict' annotations, as shown in the examples above.

4.11   Explain the concept of Spring Data repositories and how they simplify database operations.

Spring Data repositories provide a simplified way of working with databases in a Spring Framework application. A repository is essentially a collection of related data that is stored and accessed using a particular data access technology. Spring Data repositories provide a standardized way of defining and accessing repositories in your application, which helps to eliminate common boilerplate code and simplify database operations.

One of the key benefits of Spring Data repositories is that they provide a high-level abstraction layer over the underlying data access technology. This means that you can work with databases without having to write low-level SQL queries or use vendor-specific APIs. Instead, you can define the data model and repository interface using Spring Data annotations and API, and Spring will generate the necessary code to interact with the database.

For example, let's say you have a simple entity class 'User' that represents a user in your application:

```
public class User {
    private Long id;
    private String username;
    private String password;
    // getters and setters
}
```

To create a Spring Data repository for this entity, you would define an interface that extends the 'Repository' interface provided by Spring Data:

```
public interface UserRepository extends Repository<User, Long> {
  User findByUsername(String username);
}
```

The 'UserRepository' interface defines a method 'findByUser-name' that returns a 'User' instance based on the provided username. When you run your application, Spring generates the necessary code to implement this method based on the conventions defined in the method name. This means that you don't have to write any SQL queries or JDBC code to fetch the user from the database - Spring takes care of it for you.

Spring Data repositories also support a wide range of data access technologies, including JDBC, JPA, MongoDB, Redis, Cassandra, and more. This means that you can easily switch between different data stores without having to modify your application code.

In summary, Spring Data repositories simplify database operations by providing a standardized way of defining and accessing repositories in your application. They eliminate the need for boilerplate code and low-level SQL queries, making it easier to work with databases in your Spring Framework applications.

4.12 What is the purpose of the Spring Data REST project?

The Spring Data REST project is a part of the larger Spring Data project, which provides a set of abstractions and utilities for working with various data stores in a consistent and easy-to-use manner.

The main purpose of the Spring Data REST project is to provide a way to quickly and easily expose a RESTful API for any Spring Data repository. It accomplishes this by automatically creating a RESTful API for any entity managed by a Spring Data repository. This API provides standard HTTP methods for CRUD (Create, Read, Update, Delete) operations and supports querying and filtering of data.

By using Spring Data REST, developers can very quickly build a RESTful API for their application without having to write any boilerplate code. This allows them to focus on building their application logic instead of worrying about how to expose that functionality through an API.

Additionally, Spring Data REST provides a number of features that make it easy to customize the behavior and functionality of the generated API. For example, it supports customizing the URLs used for resources and relationships, as well as providing hooks for customizing the default behavior of the API.

Overall, the Spring Data REST project is a powerful tool for building RESTful APIs quickly and easily using the Spring Framework, and can save developers a significant amount of time and effort.

4.13   Explain the use of ResponseEntity and how it helps in building RESTful APIs using Spring MVC.

In Spring MVC, the ResponseEntity is used to wrap an HTTP response that can contain both the body of the response and any relevant headers. The ResponseEntity is very useful for handling HTTP responses when building RESTful APIs in Spring MVC.

With ResponseEntity, we can customize the HTTP status code, headers, and the response body. It allows us to control the HTTP response in a finer-grained manner.

Here is an example of how we can use ResponseEntity in Spring MVC:

```
@RequestMapping(value = "/products/{id}", method = RequestMethod.GET
    )
public ResponseEntity<Product> getProduct(@PathVariable("id") long
    id) {
  Product product = productService.getProductById(id);
  if (product == null) {
      return new ResponseEntity<Product>(HttpStatus.NOT_FOUND);
  }
  return new ResponseEntity<Product>(product, HttpStatus.OK);
}
```

Here, we are defining an endpoint to get a product with a given id. In this method, we are using the ProductService to retrieve the product with the given id. If the product is not found, we are returning a ResponseEntity with a HttpStatus.NOT_FOUND status code. If the product is found, we are returning a ResponseEntity with a HttpStatus.OK status code and the product as the response body.

The ResponseEntity can also be used to set the headers of the HTTP response. Here is an example:

```
@RequestMapping(value = "/products", method = RequestMethod.POST)
public ResponseEntity<Product> createProduct(@RequestBody Product
    product) {
  productService.createProduct(product);
  HttpHeaders headers = new HttpHeaders();
  headers.setLocation(URI.create("/products/" + product.getId()));
  return new ResponseEntity<Product>(headers, HttpStatus.CREATED);
}
```

Here, we are defining an endpoint to create a new product. After creating the product using the ProductService, we are setting the location header to the URI of the newly created product. We are then returning a ResponseEntity with a HttpStatus.CREATED status code and the headers we just set.

In summary, ResponseEntity is a powerful tool in Spring MVC for building RESTful APIs. It allows us to customize the HTTP response in a finer-grained manner by setting the HTTP status code, headers, and response body.

4.14   How can you handle exceptions in a Spring MVC application using @ExceptionHandler and @ControllerAdvice?

In a Spring MVC application, exceptions can be handled in a centralized manner using the '@ExceptionHandler' and '@ControllerAdvice' annotations.

'@ExceptionHandler' is an annotation used to handle exceptions thrown from a specific controller method. When an exception is thrown, Spring MVC looks for a method annotated with '@ExceptionHandler' in the controller class and invokes it.

'@ControllerAdvice' is an annotation used to define a class that provides global exception handling for all controllers. This class can contain multiple '@ExceptionHandler' methods that handle different types of exceptions.

To handle exceptions using '@ExceptionHandler' and '@ControllerAdvice', follow these steps:

1. Implement a method annotated with '@ExceptionHandler' in the controller class to handle the specific exception. For example:

```
@RestController
public class MyController {

    @ExceptionHandler(MyException.class)
    public ResponseEntity<String> handleMyException(MyException ex)
        {
        return new ResponseEntity<>("An error occurred: " + ex.
            getMessage(), HttpStatus.INTERNAL_SERVER_ERROR);
    }

    @GetMapping("/foo")
    public String foo() throws MyException {
        throw new MyException("Something went wrong");
    }
}
```

In this example, 'MyException' is a custom exception that extends 'Exception'. When the '/foo' endpoint is called, it throws 'MyException'. The 'handleMyException' method handles this exception and returns an error response.

2. Implement a class annotated with '@ControllerAdvice' to handle global exceptions. For example:

```
@ControllerAdvice
public class GlobalExceptionHandler {

    @ExceptionHandler(Exception.class)
    public ResponseEntity<String> handleException(Exception ex) {
        return new ResponseEntity<>("An error occurred: " + ex.
            getMessage(), HttpStatus.INTERNAL_SERVER_ERROR);
    }
}
```

In this example, 'GlobalExceptionHandler' is a class that handles all exceptions thrown by any controller by implementing a method annotated with '@ExceptionHandler'. The 'handle-

Exception' method handles all exceptions by returning an error response.

3. Test the exception handling by calling the controller method that throws the exception. For example, make a call to 'http://localhost:8080/foo'. In this case, the 'handleMyException' method in the controller class will handle the exception and return an error response.

If no '@ExceptionHandler' method is found in the controller class for a specific exception, Spring MVC searches for a matching method in the '@ControllerAdvice' class. If no matching method is found, Spring MVC returns a default error response.

In conclusion, using '@ExceptionHandler' and '@ControllerAdvice' is a powerful way to handle exceptions in a Spring MVC application. It allows developers to centralize exception handling logic and makes it easier to maintain and debug the application.

4.15 What is the role of the WebApplicationInitializer interface in Spring MVC?

The WebApplicationInitializer interface is used in Spring MVC to bootstrap the servlet container. This interface allows you to configure your Spring application programmatically without using any XML configuration files.

When a Spring MVC application is deployed to a servlet container, the container looks for any classes that implement the

WebApplicationInitializer interface. If it finds any, then it invokes the onStartup() method of that class, which is where you can configure your Spring application.

In the onStartup() method of a class that implements WebApplicationInitializer, you can use the Spring API to create and configure various components, such as DispatcherServlet, ServletContextListener, ServletFilters, and any other custom components that your application requires.

Here's an example of a WebApplicationInitializer implementation:

```
public class MyWebApplicationInitializer implements
    WebApplicationInitializer {

    @Override
    public void onStartup(ServletContext container) throws
        ServletException {
        AnnotationConfigWebApplicationContext context = new
            AnnotationConfigWebApplicationContext();
        context.register(MyConfig.class);

        container.addListener(new ContextLoaderListener(context));

        ServletRegistration.Dynamic dispatcher = container.addServlet
            ("dispatcher", new DispatcherServlet(context));
        dispatcher.setLoadOnStartup(1);
        dispatcher.addMapping("/");
    }
}
```

In this example, the onStartup() method creates an instance of AnnotationConfigWebApplicationContext and registers a configuration class called MyConfig. It then registers a ContextLoaderListener that will load the Spring context when the servlet container starts up. Finally, it creates and registers a DispatcherServlet and maps it to the root URL.

Overall, the WebApplicationInitializer interface plays a critical role in configuring the Spring MVC application programmatically, which provides more flexibility and control over the application's configuration than using XML configuration files.

4.16   How can you use Spring Boot's conditional annotations (@Conditional, @ConditionalOnProperty, etc.) for controlling bean creation?

Spring Boot's conditional annotations enable developers to control bean creation based on certain conditions. These annotations allow Spring Boot to dynamically decide which beans to create and which ones to skip, based on specified criteria. Lets look at some examples of how these annotations can be used for controlling bean creation.

1. @Conditional Annotation:

The '@Conditional' annotation is used to conditionally create a bean based on a certain condition(s). It accepts an array of classes that implement the 'Condition' interface. These classes define the condition(s) that must be met in order for the bean to be created.

For example, lets say we want to create a bean only if a specific environment variable is set. We can define a custom condition class called 'EnvCondition' that checks for the environment variable value. Then we can use the '@Conditional' annotation to conditionally create the bean based on this condition:

```
@Bean
@Conditional(EnvCondition.class)
public MyBean myBean() {
    // bean initialization code
```

```
}
```

2. @ConditionalOnProperty Annotation:

The '@ConditionalOnProperty' annotation is used to create a bean only if a certain configuration property is defined and has a specific value. This annotation accepts the name of the property and its expected value.

For example, if we want to create a bean only if a certain property 'myapp.enabled' is set to true, we can define our bean method like this:

```
@Bean
@ConditionalOnProperty(name = "myapp.enabled", havingValue = "true")
public MyBean myBean() {
    // bean initialization code
}
```

3. @ConditionalOnClass Annotation:

The '@ConditionalOnClass' annotation is used to create a bean only if a certain class is present in the classpath. This annotation accepts one or more fully qualified class names.

For example, if we want to create a bean only if the 'javax.servlet .Servlet' class is present in the classpath, we can define our bean method like this:

```
@Bean
@ConditionalOnClass(name = "javax.servlet.Servlet")
public MyBean myBean() {
    // bean initialization code
}
```

4. @ConditionalOnMissingBean Annotation:

The '@ConditionalOnMissingBean' annotation is used to create a bean only if no bean of the same type or with the same name already exists in the context.

For example, if we want to create a bean only if no bean with the same name 'myBean' already exists in the context, we can define our bean method like this:

```
@Bean
@ConditionalOnMissingBean(name="myBean")
public MyBean myBean() {
    // bean initialization code
}
```

Overall, Spring Boot's conditional annotations provide a powerful mechanism for developers to dynamically control bean creation. By using these annotations, we can make our code more robust and flexible, and reduce the amount of boilerplate code needed to handle different scenarios.

4.17   Explain the role of Spring Cloud in microservices architecture.

Spring Cloud is a set of tools and frameworks that helps to build distributed systems using the microservices architecture pattern. It provides a set of libraries and tools which makes it easier to develop general-purpose microservices. The use of Spring Cloud provides a lot of benefits in microservices architectures:

1. Service Discovery: In a microservices architecture, there are many services, and each service can have many instances running. Service discovery enables services to find and communicate with each other. Spring Cloud provides service discovery

tools like Eureka, Consul, and ZooKeeper.

2. Load Balancing: As there can be multiple instances of services, load balancing is required to distribute the request load among them. Spring Cloud provides a client-side load balancing library, Ribbon, which integrates with service registration and discovery tools like Eureka.

3. Configuration Management: Spring Cloud provides a centralized system that enables you to manage configuration across multiple services. It can fetch configuration data from a Git repository or from a centralized configuration server like Spring Cloud Config Server.

4. Circuit Breaking: In a distributed system, failures are common, and they can spread across services. Spring Cloud provides a circuit breaker pattern library, Hystrix, that enables services to stop sending requests to failing services and to quickly recover when they become available again.

5. API Gateway: Spring Cloud provides a gateway service for routing requests to the appropriate service instances. This is useful when having a common endpoint for multiple services.

6. Distributed Tracing: Spring Cloud provides a distributed tracing system built on top of Zipkin, which helps in tracing the execution of requests across multiple microservices.

In conclusion, Spring Cloud plays a critical role in microservices architecture by providing a set of libraries and tools that handle service discovery, load balancing, configuration management, circuit breaking, gateway service, and distributed tracing, making it easier to build and manage microservices.

4.18   What are the differences between Spring Batch and Spring Integration? When should you use each?

Spring Batch and Spring Integration are two different frameworks within the Spring ecosystem.

Spring Batch is a framework for writing batch processing jobs. It provides built-in support for common batch processing use cases such as reading data from a variety of sources, processing it in a number of stages, and then writing it back to some destination. Spring Batch is designed for large-scale batch processing and offers features such as parallel processing, job restart/retry, and transaction management.

Spring Integration, on the other hand, is a framework for building message-driven applications. It provides integration patterns and adapters for interacting with various messaging systems, such as JMS, AMQP, and MQTT. With Spring Integration, you can build event-driven applications by configuring message channels, endpoints, and filters. You can use Spring Integration to build sophisticated integration flows that integrate multiple systems, processes, and services in a loosely-coupled and modular fashion.

To summarize, Spring Batch is suitable for processing large volumes of data in a batch-oriented fashion, while Spring Integration is more suitable for integrating different systems and services by orchestrating message-driven interactions.

Here's an example of when to use each:

Suppose you have an application that needs to import a large amount of data from a file on a regular basis (e.g., nightly). In this case, Spring Batch would be a good fit as it provides all the necessary features for reading the data, processing it, and writing it to a database. Additionally, Spring Batch provides advanced features like parallel processing, chunking, and error handling which makes it perfect for handling large volumes of data.

Alternatively, suppose you have a distributed system with multiple services that need to communicate with each other. In this case, Spring Integration provides a convenient and flexible way to orchestrate message-driven interactions between the various services using a variety of messaging protocols. With Spring Integration, you can configure various channels, endpoints, and filters to build a fault-tolerant and decoupled system that can scale up or down depending on your needs.

4.19 What is Spring WebFlux, and how does it enable reactive programming in Spring applications?

Spring WebFlux is one of the most significant additions to the Spring Framework that enables reactive programming in Spring applications. Spring WebFlux is a reactive-stack web framework that includes support for reactive programming, which is a programming paradigm that is designed to handle asynchronous and non-blocking I/O efficiently.

Reactive programming is focused on building responsive, resilient, and scalable applications that can handle a large number of concurrent users with less resource consumption. The reactive approach differs from traditional, imperative programming models that rely on blocking I/O and thread-per-request architectures, which hinder performance and scalability under high loads.

Spring WebFlux leverages the reactive core library of Reactor to enable non-blocking, event-driven programming, suitable for developing high-performance and scalable web applications. Reactor is based on the Reactive Streams specification, which enables interoperability between reactive streams frameworks.

Spring WebFlux provides several essential features, including reactive HTTP and WebSocket clients, support for functional endpoints, and a flexible reactive programming model for building reactive web applications.

The framework's core philosophy is centered around functional programming principles that are designed to promote a declarative, reactive programming style. Spring WebFlux uses the Project Reactor library to provide reactive programming constructs, including Flux and Mono classes.

Flux represents a reactive stream of 0..N elements, while Mono is a reactive type that represents 0..1 elements. With these reactive types, developers can compose async and non-blocking flows of data and handle errors and timeouts. These types can also provide a more intuitive and expressive method of handling errors and results compared to traditional imperative programming.

Overall, Spring WebFlux provides a powerful set of reactive programming tools and constructs that enable developers to build scalable, high-performance web applications that can handle a large number of concurrent users without putting unnecessary strain on the system's resources.

4.20 How can you handle file uploads in a Spring MVC application?

Java Spring MVC provides built-in mechanisms for handling file uploads that allow users to upload files to web applications. Spring MVC has a multipart resolver that is used to handle file uploads.

Here are the steps to handle file uploads in a Spring MVC application:

1. Add the following dependencies to your Maven or Gradle build file:

```
<dependency>
    <groupId>org.springframework</groupId>
    <artifactId>spring-webmvc</artifactId>
    <version>{spring-version}</version>
</dependency>
<dependency>
    <groupId>commons-fileupload</groupId>
    <artifactId>commons-fileupload</artifactId>
    <version>{commons-fileupload-version}</version>
</dependency>
```

2. Configure the multipart resolver in your Spring configuration file:

```
<bean id="multipartResolver" class="org.springframework.web.
    multipart.commons.CommonsMultipartResolver">
    <property name="maxUploadSize" value="10485760"/>
</bean>
```

The maxUploadSize property is used to set the maximum upload file size in bytes.

3. Create a controller method to handle file uploads:

```
@RequestMapping(value = "/upload", method = RequestMethod.POST)
public String handleFileUpload(@RequestParam("file") MultipartFile
    file) throws IOException {
    // logic to handle file upload
    return "uploadSuccess";
}
```

In this example, the @RequestParam annotation is used to bind the uploaded file to a MultipartFile object.

4. Create a HTML form to upload files:

```
<form method="POST" enctype="multipart/form-data" action="/upload">
    <input type="file" name="file"/><br/><br/>
    <input type="submit" value="Upload"/>
</form>
```

The enctype attribute is set to "multipart/form-data" to enable file uploads.

That's it! With these steps, you can handle file uploads in Spring MVC.

Chapter 5

Expert

5.1 Explain how the ApplicationContext hierarchy works in Spring, and how it can be used for multi-module applications.

The ApplicationContext hierarchy in Spring provides a way to structure your application using multiple contexts with a parent-child relationship. This can be useful in large-scale or multi-module applications where you may want to divide your application into smaller, more manageable sections that can be configured independently.

At the core of this hierarchy is the root application context, which serves as the parent context for all other contexts in the hierarchy. Each child context can access all the beans and resources of its parent context, but the parent context cannot access any beans or resources of its child contexts.

When it comes to multi-module applications, each module can have its own child application context that is a sub-context of the main application context. For example, if you have a web application with multiple modules like API, Auth, and Database, each can have its own configurable child context. You can define the configurations for each module, including its beans, properties, and other resources, in their respective child contexts.

When loading these child contexts in Spring, the hierarchy is set up so that the root application context is loaded first, followed by the child contexts. This means that the beans in the root context are available to all child contexts, but beans defined in a child context are not directly exposed to other child contexts.

To take advantage of ApplicationContext hierarchy in Spring, you can simply create a parent-child relationship and configure each context as you would normally. Here's an example of how this can be done:

```
// Create a new root context
AbstractApplicationContext parentContext = new
    AnnotationConfigApplicationContext();
parentContext.refresh();

// Create the child context for the API module
AbstractApplicationContext childContext = new
    AnnotationConfigApplicationContext();
childContext.setParent(parentContext);
childContext.register(ApiConfig.class);
childContext.refresh();

// Create the child context for the Auth module
AbstractApplicationContext authContext = new
    AnnotationConfigApplicationContext();
authContext.setParent(parentContext);
authContext.register(AuthConfig.class);
authContext.refresh();
```

In this example, we create a root context using the AnnotationConfigApplicationContext class, which allows us to configure the context using Java-based configuration. We then create two child contexts, one for the API module and one for the Auth module, and set the parent context for each. Finally, we register the configuration classes for each child context and refresh the contexts.

By using ApplicationContext hierarchy in Spring, we can build modular, scalable, and more maintainable applications.

5.2 How can you implement custom property sources and property source placeholders in Spring?

Custom property sources and property source placeholders are powerful features in the Spring Framework that allow us to externalize configuration details of our application. They make the application more flexible and easier to maintain, as configuration values can be changed without making any changes in the underlying code.

Here's how you can implement custom property sources and property source placeholders in Spring:

Custom Property Sources

Spring provides an interface called 'PropertySource' that allows us to define custom property sources. Essentially, a 'PropertySource' is a key/value pair that can be used to provide configuration properties to different parts of our application. We can create our custom 'PropertySource' implementation by implementing this interface and overriding the 'getProperty(String name)' method to return a property value for a given name.

```
public class MyPropertySource implements PropertySource<String> {

    private final Properties properties;

    public MyPropertySource() {
        properties = new Properties();
        // populate properties
        properties.put("my.property.key", "my.property.value");
        // add more properties
    }

    @Override
    public String getName() {
        return "myPropertySource";
    }

    @Override
    public Object getProperty(String name) {
        return properties.getProperty(name);
    }
}
```

In the above example, we have defined a custom 'PropertySource' called 'MyPropertySource' that has a predefined key/value pair. We can register this property source with the Spring 'Environment' using the 'StandardEnvironment' class.

```
@Configuration
public class AppConfig {

    @Bean
    public MyPropertySource myPropertySource() {
        return new MyPropertySource();
    }

    @Bean
    public static PropertySourcesPlaceholderConfigurer
        propertySourcesPlaceholderConfigurer() {
        final PropertySourcesPlaceholderConfigurer configurer = new
            PropertySourcesPlaceholderConfigurer();
        configurer.setPropertySources(new MutablePropertySources()
            .addFirst(new StandardEnvironment().getPropertySources
                ())
            .addFirst(myPropertySource()));
        return configurer;
    }
```

```
}
```

In the above configuration, we have defined a 'PropertySource-sPlaceholderConfigurer' bean that is responsible for replacing placeholders in property values with their actual values. We have also added our custom 'PropertySource' to the 'PropertySources' object. Note that we have added our custom 'PropertySource' before 'StandardEnvironment' to give it higher priority.

Property Source Placeholders

Spring's 'PropertySourcesPlaceholderConfigurer' enables property placeholders in bean definitions, which means that we can use properties in our beans by defining a property placeholder. This placeholder is replaced with the actual property value at runtime.

```
@Value("${property.key}")
private String propertyValue;
```

In the above example, '$property.key' is the property placeholder. The actual property value for this placeholder can be defined in different property sources, such as environment variables, system properties, or custom property sources.

We can also use expressions in a property value by enclosing them in '#'.

```
@Value("#{myBean.someMethod()}")
private String propertyValue;
```

In the above example, '#myBean.someMethod()' is an expression that calls a method on the 'myBean' bean and returns its result.

In conclusion, custom property sources and property source placeholders provide an efficient way to externalize configuration details in a Spring application. We can define our custom property sources by implementing the 'PropertySources' interface and register them with the Spring 'Environment'. Additionally, Spring's 'PropertySourcesPlaceholderConfigurer' enables us to use property placeholders in bean definitions and replace them with their actual values at runtime.

5.3   Explain how Spring supports AspectJ-based AOP in addition to its proxy-based AOP.

Spring supports two approaches to AOP: proxy-based AOP and AspectJ-based AOP. Both approaches can be used interchangeably, and Spring provides support for both, allowing developers to choose the most suitable approach for their application needs.

Proxy-based AOP is a runtime AOP solution where a proxy object intercepts the method calls, based on the advice configured, before delegating the call to the target object. This makes AOP possible without requiring modifications to the original codebase. In Spring, this type of AOP is achieved by creating a proxy object around the target object, which implements the same interfaces as the target object, and intercepts the method calls based on the advice configured.

AspectJ-based AOP is a compile-time AOP solution that uses a special syntax to declare and weave cross-cutting concerns into a Java class. With AspectJ, the aspects are defined as regular Java classes with advice and pointcuts. Pointcuts are used to define the set of join points where the advice should be applied. The AspectJ compiler then applies the aspects to the Java class bytecodes during compilation.

To support AspectJ-based AOP, Spring provides both runtime and compile-time weaving options. In runtime weaving, Spring uses an AspectJ weaver to dynamically weave aspects into the target object through a proxy. This approach allows AspectJ-based AOP to be used in an existing Spring application without requiring any modifications to the application or build process.

In contrast, compile-time weaving requires a special build process where AspectJ aspects are compiled and woven into the Java class bytecodes at compile-time. Spring provides a set of Gradle and Maven plugins that can be used to automate the AspectJ weaving process during the build.

In conclusion, Spring supports both proxy-based and AspectJ-based AOP, providing developers with flexibility and options to choose the most appropriate approach for their application needs. Proxy-based AOP is a runtime solution that allows AOP without requiring modifications to the original code, while AspectJ-based AOP is a compile-time solution that allows for more fine-grained control and performance optimization.

5.4   How can you implement custom AOP advice types in Spring?

In Spring, AOP (Aspect-Oriented Programming) is implemented using advice, joinpoints, and pointcuts. Spring allows for creating custom AOP advice types to extend its existing capabilities of providing Before, After and Around advice to the application.

To implement custom AOP advice types in Spring, you can
follow the following approach:

1. Create a class that implements the interface 'org.springframe-
work.aop.Advice', which is the base interface for all types of
advice in Spring AOP.

2. Implement the required behavior based on the specific use
case of the custom advice type. For example, if you want to
implement a custom logging advice, you might override the
'org.springframework.aop.MethodBeforeAdvice' interface to log
the method entry before the advised method is called.

3. Annotate the custom advice type class with '@Aspect' annotation to indicate that this class is an AOP aspect. This will
allow Spring to recognize the custom advice type as an AOP
aspect.

4. Define a pointcut that specifies the joinpoints where the
custom advice should be applied. You can define the pointcut
using the '@Pointcut' annotation on a method that returns a
'org.aspectj.lang.annotation.Pointcut' object.

5. Finally, declare the custom advice type as a bean in the
Spring application context so that Spring can manage its lifecycle.

Here is an example of a custom AOP advice that logs the
method execution time:

```
import org.aspectj.lang.JoinPoint;
import org.aspectj.lang.annotation.Aspect;
import org.aspectj.lang.annotation.Before;
import org.springframework.aop.MethodBeforeAdvice;
```

```
@Aspect
public class ExecutionTimeAdvice implements MethodBeforeAdvice {

    @Before("execution(*␣com.example.service.*.*(..))")
    public void before(JoinPoint joinPoint) throws Throwable {
        long startTime = System.currentTimeMillis();
        // Proceed with the advised method
        joinPoint.proceed();
        long endTime = System.currentTimeMillis();
        System.out.println("Execution␣time␣of␣" + joinPoint.
            getSignature().getName() + "␣method:␣"
                + (endTime - startTime) + "ms");
    }
}
```

In this example, we use the '@Aspect' annotation to declare the
class as an AOP aspect. We then override the 'before' method of
the 'MethodBeforeAdvice' interface to log the method execution
time. The 'execution' expression in the '@Before' annotation
specifies the pointcut where this advice should be applied.

Once you have defined the custom AOP advice, you can declare
it as a bean in the Spring application context, as shown below:

```
<bean id="executionTimeAdvice" class="com.example.aop.
    ExecutionTimeAdvice"/>
```

By declaring the bean in the application context, you make it
available for Spring to use for advice on appropriate pointcuts.

5.5   How can you handle distributed trans-actions in Spring using the Java Trans-action API (JTA)?

When dealing with distributed applications, there might be a
need for coordinating transactions across multiple data sources

or microservices. Spring provides support for distributed transactions using the Java Transaction API (JTA) by enabling you
to configure and manage transaction managers that can handle
multiple resources and their transactions.

To handle distributed transactions in Spring using JTA, the
following steps can be taken:

Step 1: Configure TransactionManager Spring requires a
transaction manager to handle distributed transactions. The
JTA transaction manager can support multiple resources, including databases and message queues. In Spring, the JTA
transaction manager can be configured using the 'JtaTransactionManager' class which can be created and configured as a
bean in the Spring application context. The 'UserTransaction'
and 'TransactionManager' interface provided by the JTA API
are used by the 'JtaTransactionManager' to interact with the
underlying transaction manager.

Example:

```
<bean id="transactionManager" class="org.springframework.transaction
    .jta.JtaTransactionManager">
  <property name="transactionManagerName" value="java:/
      TransactionManager"/>
  <property name="userTransactionName" value="java:jboss/
      UserTransaction"/>
</bean>
```

Step 2: Define Multiple Data Sources For distributed transactions, multiple data sources that are part of the same transaction will be involved. In Spring, multiple data sources can be
defined and configured using the 'DataSource' interface, which
can be injected as beans into your transactional services. Spring
also provides a variety of data access templates, like 'JdbcTemplate', etc., that can be used in conjunction with the 'Data-
Source'.

Example:

```
<bean id="datasource1" class="org.apache.commons.dbcp2.
    BasicDataSource">
  <property name="driverClassName" value="com.mysql.jdbc.Driver"/>
  <property name="url" value="jdbc:mysql://localhost/db1"/>
  <property name="username" value="root"/>
  <property name="password" value="password"/>
</bean>

<bean id="datasource2" class="org.apache.commons.dbcp2.
    BasicDataSource">
  <property name="driverClassName" value="com.mysql.jdbc.Driver"/>
  <property name="url" value="jdbc:mysql://localhost/db2"/>
  <property name="username" value="root"/>
  <property name="password" value="password"/>
</bean>
```

Step 3: Define the Transactional Service In Spring, transactional services are annotated with the '@Transactional' annotation. The '@Transactional' annotation can be applied at the method level or at the class level. This annotation tells Spring to manage the transactional behavior of the annotated service.

Example:

```
@Transactional
@Service
public class MyService {

    @Autowired
    private JdbcTemplate jdbc1;

    @Autowired
    private JdbcTemplate jdbc2;

    public void performDistributedTransaction() {
        jdbc1.execute("INSERT INTO TABLE1 (ID, NAME) VALUES (1, '
            Name1')");
        jdbc2.execute("INSERT INTO TABLE2 (ID, NAME) VALUES (1, '
            Name2')");
    }
}
```

Step 4: Use the Transactional Service In the final step, the transactional service can be deployed and invoked to execute the distributed transaction.

Example:

```
@Autowired
MyService myService;

public void executeDistributedTransaction() {
    myService.performDistributedTransaction();
}
```

In conclusion, configuring and managing distributed transactions with JTA in Spring is relatively simple, especially when using Spring's built-in transaction management capabilities. By configuring a JTA transaction manager, defining multiple data sources, and annotating transactional services with '@Transactional' annotation, Spring can handle distributed transactions across multiple resources in a single coordinated transaction.

5.6   What are the strategies for handling concurrency in Spring Batch applications?

Spring Batch offers various ways to handle concurrency in its applications depending on the need of the application. Here are some of the strategies for handling concurrency in Spring Batch applications:

1. Task Execution: Spring Batch provides a TaskExecutor interface that can be used to execute tasks in a concurrent manner. The default implementation of TaskExecutor is SimpleAsyncTaskExecutor which can be configured to execute tasks using a pool of threads.

Example:

```
@Bean
public TaskExecutor taskExecutor() {
    ThreadPoolTaskExecutor executor = new ThreadPoolTaskExecutor();
    executor.setMaxPoolSize(10);
    executor.setQueueCapacity(25);
    return executor;
}
```

2. Scaling: Spring Batch provides a scaling mechanism that enables the horizontal scaling of a job. This approach involves splitting a large job into smaller tasks and executing them concurrently on multiple threads.

Example:

```
@Bean
public Step step1() {
    return stepBuilderFactory.get("step1")
        .<String, String>chunk(10)
        .reader(reader())
        .processor(processor())
        .writer(writer())
        .taskExecutor(taskExecutor())
        .build();
}
```

3. Partitioning: Another way to handle concurrency is by partitioning the data and processing them on multiple threads. This approach is useful when processing a large dataset.

Example:

```
@Bean
@StepScope
public ItemReader<Person> partitionedReader(@Value("#{
    stepExecutionContext['partition']}") int partition) {
    JdbcPagingItemReader<Person> reader = new JdbcPagingItemReader
        <>();
    reader.setDataSource(dataSource);
    reader.setFetchSize(10);
    reader.setRowMapper(new PersonRowMapper());
    reader.setQueryProvider(createQueryProvider());
    reader.setParameterValues(Collections.singletonMap("partition",
        partition));
    return reader;
```

```
}
```

4. Synchronization: Spring Batch provides a synchronization mechanism that can be used to synchronize access to shared resources like files or databases.

Example:

```
@Bean
@StepScope
public ItemWriter<Person> writer() {
    SynchronizedItemStreamWriter<Person> writer = new
        SynchronizedItemStreamWriter<>();
    writer.setDelegate(new FlatFileItemWriterBuilder<Person>()
        .name("personItemWriter")
        .resource(new FileSystemResource("output/persons.csv"))
        .delimited()
        .names(new String[]{"firstName", "lastName"})
        .build());
    writer.setMutex(new SpelExpressionParser().parseExpression("
        stepExecution.jobExecution.executionContext"));
    return writer;
}
```

By using one or more of these concurrency strategies, Spring Batch applications can handle large volumes of data efficiently and ensure data consistency.

5.7   How can you integrate Spring Security with OAuth2 and OpenID Connect for securing RESTful APIs?

Spring Security provides comprehensive support for OAuth2 and OpenID Connect-based security solutions.

Here are the steps on how to integrate Spring Security with OAuth2 and OpenID Connect for securing RESTful APIs:

1. Add the required dependencies - The first step is to add the
following dependencies to your Spring Boot application:

```
implementation 'org.springframework.boot:spring-boot-starter-
    security'
implementation 'org.springframework.security:spring-security-oauth2-
    client'
implementation 'org.springframework.security:spring-security-oauth2-
    jose'
```

2. Configure the OAuth2 client - After adding the dependencies,
configure the OAuth2 client by specifying the authorization
server's details in the 'application.yml' or 'application.proper-
ties' file. For example:

```
spring:
  security:
    oauth2:
      client:
        registration:
          okta:
            clientId: <client_id>
            clientSecret: <client_secret>
            scope:
              - openid
              - profile
              - email
        provider:
          okta:
            issuerUri: https://dev-123456.okta.com/oauth2/default
```

3. Configure the security filter chain - The next step is to
configure Spring Security's filter chain to include the OAuth2
security filter. This filter intercepts requests and validates the
OAuth2 access token before allowing the request to proceed.
This can be done using the 'WebSecurityConfigurerAdapter'
class, for example:

```
@Configuration
@EnableWebSecurity
public class SecurityConfig extends WebSecurityConfigurerAdapter {

    @Override
    protected void configure(HttpSecurity http) throws Exception {
        http.authorizeRequests(authorizeRequests ->
            authorizeRequests.antMatchers("/api/**").authenticated())
            .oauth2ResourceServer(OAuth2ResourceServerConfigurer::jwt)
            ;
```

```
    }
  }
```

In this example, any requests to '/api/**' paths are authenticated, and the 'OAuth2ResourceServerConfigurer' is used to configure JWT-based security for the OAuth2 resource server.

4. Secure your REST endpoints - Finally, secure your RESTful endpoints by adding the '@PreAuthorize' annotation to your REST controller methods. For example:

```
@RestController
@RequestMapping("/api")
public class MyRestController {

    @GetMapping("/resource")
    @PreAuthorize("hasAuthority('SCOPE_profile')")
    public String getResource() {
        return "Hello,␣World!";
    }
}
```

Here, the '@PreAuthorize' annotation is used to restrict access to the '/api/resource' endpoint to users with the 'SCOPE_profile' authority in their access token.

In summary, integrating Spring Security with OAuth2 and OpenID Connect for securing RESTful APIs involves adding the necessary dependencies, configuring the OAuth2 client, configuring the security filter chain, and securing your REST endpoints using the '@PreAuthorize' annotation.

5.8   Explain the concept of the Spring Session project and its role in managing user sessions across multiple instances of an application.

Spring Session is a project within the Spring ecosystem that provides session management functionality for web applications. It helps in managing user sessions across multiple instances of an application. The Spring Session project provides a consistent programming and configuration model for session management.

In a distributed web application, there are often multiple instances of the application running simultaneously to handle user requests. Traditional session management will tie a user session to a specific instance of the application. This means that if the user needs to be redirected to a different application instance for some reason (such as load balancing), the session data will be lost, leading to a poor user experience.

Spring Session addresses this problem by externalizing session state from the application container and managing it in a central location using either a relational database or NoSQL data store. This allows the session data to be accessed by any instance of the application, providing a shared session context across multiple instances.

Spring Session provides a simple API for managing sessions, including the ability to retrieve, create, and delete sessions. It also provides support for a variety of session-related tasks, such as session expiration, attribute updates, and session invalidation.

To use Spring Session in your application, you need to first configure it with a data store. Spring Session has built-in support
for several popular data stores, including Redis, MongoDB, and
JDBC. Once you have configured the data store, you can use
the Spring Session API to manage user sessions.

Here is an example of configuring Spring Session with Redis:

```
@Configuration
@EnableRedisHttpSession(maxInactiveIntervalInSeconds = 1800)
public class RedisSessionConfig {

  @Bean
  public JedisConnectionFactory connectionFactory() {
    return new JedisConnectionFactory();
  }
}
```

This code configures Spring Session to use Redis as the data
store for session management. It also sets the maximum session
inactive interval to 1800 seconds (30 minutes).

In conclusion, Spring Session helps in managing user sessions
across multiple instances of an application by externalizing session state from the application container and managing it in a
central location using a data store. It provides a simple API for
managing sessions, and it supports a variety of session-related
tasks.

5.9   How can you use Spring Boot's Test support to create integration tests for your application?

Spring Boot's Test support provides a convenient way to create
integration tests for your application. Here are the steps you

can follow to create integration tests using Spring Boot:

1. Add the 'spring-boot-starter-test' dependency to your project's build file (pom.xml for Maven or build.gradle for Gradle).

```
<dependency>
    <groupId>org.springframework.boot</groupId>
    <artifactId>spring-boot-starter-test</artifactId>
</dependency>
```

2. Create a test class for your application by annotating it with '@SpringBootTest'. This annotation loads your entire application context for testing.

```
@SpringBootTest
public class MyApplicationIntegrationTest {
    // Test methods
}
```

3. Use Spring Boot's 'TestRestTemplate' to make HTTP requests to your application. 'TestRestTemplate' is a special version of 'RestTemplate' that is configured for testing. "' @RunWith(SpringRunner.class) @SpringBootTest(webEnvironment = SpringBootTest.WebEnvironment.RANDOM_PORT) public class MyApplicationIntegrationTest @Autowired private TestRestTemplate restTemplate;

@Test public void testGetHelloWorld() String response = restTemplate.getForObject("/hello", String.class); assertEquals("Hello World", response);   "'

4. You can also use 'MockMvc' to test your application's controllers. 'MockMvc' provides a way to simulate HTTP requests and test the behavior of your controllers without making actual HTTP requests.

```
@RunWith(SpringRunner.class)
@SpringBootTest
```

```
@AutoConfigureMockMvc
public class MyControllerIntegrationTest {
    @Autowired
    private MockMvc mockMvc;

    @Test
    public void testGetHelloWorld() throws Exception {
        mockMvc.perform(get("/hello"))
            .andExpect(status().isOk())
            .andExpect(content().string("Hello␣World"));
    }
}
```

5. You can also use Spring Boot's database testing support to test your application's database interactions. Spring Boot can automatically set up an in-memory database for testing, or it can use your application's configured database.

```
@RunWith(SpringRunner.class)
@SpringBootTest
@DataJpaTest
public class MyRepositoryIntegrationTest {
    @Autowired
    private TestEntityManager entityManager;

    @Autowired
    private MyRepository myRepository;

    @Test
    public void testFindAll() {
        MyEntity myEntity = new MyEntity();
        myEntity.setName("Test");
        entityManager.persist(myEntity);
        entityManager.flush();

        List<MyEntity> myEntities = myRepository.findAll();
        assertThat(myEntities).hasSize(1);
        assertThat(myEntities.get(0).getName()).isEqualTo("Test");
    }
}
```

In summary, Spring Boot's Test support provides a range of tools and annotations to create integration tests for your application, including 'TestRestTemplate', 'MockMvc', and database testing support. With these tools, you can thoroughly test your application and ensure that it works as expected in a production environment.

5.10 Explain how Spring Integration works, and how it can be used for implementing Enterprise Integration Patterns (EIP).

Spring Integration is a lightweight framework that is primarily used for implementing Enterprise Integration Patterns (EIP). EIP is a set of design patterns for integrating different systems in a software application. It can help to simplify the process of integrating different systems and technologies by providing a set of reusable patterns for common integration tasks.

At its core, Spring Integration is a messaging framework that provides a set of building blocks for constructing complex integration flows. At the heart of Spring Integration is the concept of a message channel, which is a virtual path through which messages can flow between different components in a software application. Messages are objects that contain data, and they can be anything from a simple string to a complex data structure.

In Spring Integration, messages are sent and received by message endpoints, which are responsible for processing the messages. Endpoints can be either message producers or message consumers, and they can be configured to perform a wide range of tasks, such as transforming messages, aggregating messages, filtering messages, routing messages, and so on.

Spring Integration provides a wide range of different endpoint types that can be used to build up complex integration flows, including:

- Transformers, which can be used to convert messages from one form to another

- Filters, which can be used to discard unwanted messages

- Routers, which can be used to route messages to different endpoints based on their content

- Splitters and aggregators, which can be used to break up messages into smaller pieces and then reassemble them later

- Adapters, which can be used to connect to external systems using different protocols, such as JMS, FTP, HTTP, and more.

Spring Integration provides a wide range of different channel types that can be used to route messages between different endpoints, including:

- Direct channels, which are used for point-to-point messaging

- Publish-subscribe channels, which are used for broadcasting messages to multiple endpoints

- Priority channels, which are used to prioritize messages based on their content or other criteria.

In addition to these endpoints and channels, Spring Integration provides a number of other features that can be used to monitor and manage messages as they flow through the system. For example, it provides support for message tracing, error handling, and transaction management, among other things.

To use Spring Integration for implementing EIP, you simply need to select the appropriate endpoint and channel types for your particular integration scenario, and then configure them to work together in a cohesive way. For example, if you were building an integration flow that needed to consume messages from an external message queue using JMS, you might start by configuring a JMS adapter to connect to the message queue. You could then use a transformer to convert the incoming messages from their JMS-specific format into something more consumable by other components in your system. Finally, you might send the transformed message through a direct channel to another endpoint that would handle further processing, such as message routing, filtering, or aggregation.

In summary, Spring Integration is a powerful and flexible framework that can be used to implement a wide range of Enterprise Integration Patterns in a software application. It provides a set of building blocks, including message endpoints and channels, that can be combined in various ways to create complex integration flows. Overall, Spring Integration is an excellent choice for any developer who needs to integrate different systems or technologies into existing software applications.

5.11 How can you handle WebSocket communication in a Spring application using Spring WebSocket?

Spring WebSocket is a part of the Spring Framework that enables WebSocket communication between the client and the server. In order to handle WebSocket communication in a Spring application, we need to follow these steps:

1. Add the Spring WebSocket dependency to the project. This can be done by adding the following dependency to the projects pom.xml file:

```
<dependency>
```

```
      <groupId>org.springframework</groupId>
      <artifactId>spring-websocket</artifactId>
      <version>5.x.x</version>
   </dependency>
```

2. Create a WebSocket configuration class. This class should extend the 'AbstractWebSocketMessageBrokerConfigurer' class and override its 'registerStompEndpoints()' method. This method is responsible for configuring the WebSocket endpoints that the clients can connect to. Heres an example of how a WebSocket configuration class can be set up:

```
@Configuration
@EnableWebSocketMessageBroker
public class WebSocketConfig extends
     AbstractWebSocketMessageBrokerConfigurer {

   @Override
   public void configureMessageBroker(MessageBrokerRegistry config)
        {
      config.enableSimpleBroker("/topic");
      config.setApplicationDestinationPrefixes("/app");
   }

   @Override
   public void registerStompEndpoints(StompEndpointRegistry
        registry) {
      registry.addEndpoint("/websocket").withSockJS();
   }

}
```

This configuration sets up two message routes: '/topic' and '/app'. The '/topic' route is used for broadcasting messages to all connected clients, while the '/app' route is used for sending messages to a specific client.

3. Handle WebSocket messages in controllers. In order to handle WebSocket messages, we need to use Springs WebSocketHandler methods. These methods are used for sending, receiving, and processing WebSocket messages. Heres an example of how a controller can be set up to handle incoming WebSocket

messages:

```
@Controller
public class WebSocketController {

    @MessageMapping("/hello")
    @SendTo("/topic/greetings")
    public Greeting greeting(HelloMessage message) throws Exception
        {
        Thread.sleep(1000); // simulated delay
        return new Greeting("Hello,␣" + message.getName() + "!");
    }

}
```

This controller handles incoming messages on the '/hello' route and sends a response message to the '/topic/greetings' route.

4. Connect to the WebSocket endpoint from a client. Once the WebSocket endpoint has been set up and the messages have been handled in the controller, we can connect to the endpoint from a client. This can be done using a WebSocket client library or by using the built-in JavaScript library. Heres an example of how a client can connect to the endpoint using JavaScript:

```
var socket = new SockJS('/websocket');
var stompClient = Stomp.over(socket);

stompClient.connect({}, function(frame) {
    stompClient.subscribe('/topic/greetings', function(greeting) {
        var body = JSON.parse(greeting.body);
        alert(body.content);
    });
});

function sendGreeting() {
    var name = $('#name').val();
    stompClient.send("/app/hello", {}, JSON.stringify({ 'name': name
        }));
}
```

This JavaScript code creates a SockJS instance and connects to the '/websocket' endpoint. Once the connection is established, it subscribes to the '/topic/greetings' route and listens for mes-

sages. The 'sendGreeting()' function sends a message to the
'/app/hello' route when the button is clicked.

These are the basic steps required for handling WebSocket communication in a Spring application using Spring WebSocket.
With this setup, we can create real-time applications that can
handle user interactions in a seamless, responsive, and efficient
way.

5.12   What is the role of Spring Cloud Config in managing configurations for distributed applications?

In a distributed application environment, it can be challenging to maintain and manage configurations for each instance of
the application. This is where Spring Cloud Config comes in,
it provides a centralized and version-controlled mechanism for
managing configurations for distributed applications.

Spring Cloud Config allows us to externalize configurations of
our applications, which includes everything that can be part
of an application such as database configuration, connection
properties, logging configuration, and other related settings.
By externalizing configuration, we can change the configuration without deploying the application again.

Spring Cloud Config stores configurations in a Git repository,
which means it is versioned, auditable, and can be updated
easily. The configuration files are usually stored in a centralized
server, where all applications access the server to retrieve their
respective configuration files.

Additionally, Spring Cloud Config provides a mechanism called "refresh scope" which allows us to reload configurations for our application while the application is still running. This is beneficial when we want to update some configurations without restarting the application, which can lead to downtime.

Here's an example of how Spring Cloud Config works:

Let's consider a scenario where we have a microservice application running, and it connects to a PostgreSQL database. The database configuration is part of the application configurations. We can externalize the database configuration to Spring Cloud Config by creating a file named "application.yml" or "application.properties" and storing it in the Git repository.

The microservice application will then read the configuration from the Spring Cloud Config server, which can be located remotely. We can also ensure that each instance of the microservice application uses the same configuration, and any updates to the Git repository would reflect across all instances.

In conclusion, Spring Cloud Config provides a reliable and consistent mechanism for managing configurations for distributed applications. By centralizing configuration, it offers versioning, auditing, and the flexibility to update configurations without deploying the application again.

5.13   Explain how Spring Cloud Netflix can be used for service discovery, load balancing, and fault tolerance in microservices architecture.

Spring Cloud Netflix is a set of libraries that provides out-of-the-box solutions for common microservices patterns using Netflix OSS technologies. The three key capabilities that Spring Cloud Netflix provides are service discovery, load balancing, and fault tolerance.

Service Discovery In a microservices architecture, there can be many instances of a service running across different nodes, which can make it difficult to identify and communicate with instances that are currently available. Service discovery helps to overcome this problem by registering available instances of a service and providing a mechanism to look up those instances.

Spring Cloud Netflix provides Netflix Eureka Server for service discovery. Service instances register with Eureka Server and Eureka Server then maintains a registry of all available instances. When a client requests a service, it queries Eureka Server to find the available instances of the service and then uses the load balancing mechanism to choose one of those instances.

Load Balancing In a microservices architecture, there can be multiple instances of a service running at the same time. Load balancing helps distribute requests evenly across all instances of a service to prevent overloading any one instance.

Spring Cloud Netflix provides two different load balancing mechanisms: Ribbon and Eureka.

Netflix Ribbon is a client-side load balancer that can be used to load balance requests across multiple instances of a service. Ribbon is integrated with Eureka Server and can use the service registry to look up available instances of a service.

Spring Cloud Netflix also provides server-side load balancing using Netflix Zuul. Zuul is a proxy server that can route requests to appropriate service instances based on pre-defined rules.

Fault Tolerance In a microservices architecture, failures can occur at any time, which can cause a service to become unavailable or unresponsive. Fault tolerance mechanisms help to ensure the service remains available and responsive in the event of a failure.

Spring Cloud Netflix provides two fault-tolerance mechanisms: Hystrix and Turbine.

Netflix Hystrix is a library that provides a circuit breaker pattern. Hystrix can detect failures and fallback to an alternative response or service when needed. It can also monitor the health of dependent services and circuit breakers can be opened to prevent a cascading failure.

Netflix Turbine provides a consolidated dashboard view of all Hystrix streams in the system, allowing teams to monitor the health of their services in a single view.

In conclusion, Spring Cloud Netflix provides a set of libraries and tools to simplify service discovery, load balancing, and fault tolerance in microservices architecture. With Spring Cloud Netflix, you can easily build robust, scalable, and resilient microservices applications.

5.14   What is Spring Cloud Gateway, and how does it help in implementing API Gateway patterns?

Spring Cloud Gateway is an open-source, light-weight API Gateway that provides a simple way to route, filter, and enhance HTTP requests to services or applications. It is built on top of Spring Boot and offers a reactive and non-blocking architecture for handling edge service requests.

API Gateway pattern is a common architectural pattern used in microservices-based architectures to provide a single entry point for external clients to access the microservices. It acts as a gatekeeper and routes all incoming requests to the appropriate microservices, ensures security, and provides functionalities like rate limiting, authentication, and data transformation.

Spring Cloud Gateway is designed specifically for implementing the API Gateway pattern. The following are some ways it helps in achieving that:

1. Routing: Spring Cloud Gateway provides a simple and flexible mechanism for routing incoming requests to the appropriate microservices based on the URL, headers, and other information in the request. It uses the industry-standard Spring WebFlux routing mechanism that allows developers to configure the routing rules in a declarative and easy-to-understand manner.

2. Filtering: Spring Cloud Gateway also provides built-in filters to modify and enhance the incoming requests before they reach the microservices. Filters can perform tasks like authentication, rate limiting, and data transformation, making it easy to implement cross-cutting concerns in a central place.

3. Load Balancing: Spring Cloud Gateway also supports load balancing across multiple instances of a service, enabling high availability and scalability for microservices.

4. Security: Spring Cloud Gateway provides easy-to-use security integrations that allow developers to configure authentication and authorisation for their microservices.

In summary, Spring Cloud Gateway is a versatile and powerful API Gateway tool that makes it easy to implement API Gateway patterns in microservices-based architectures. It provides a simple and flexible way to route, filter, and enhance requests, while also supporting advanced features like load balancing and security integrations.

5.15   How can you implement event-driven architecture in a Spring application using Spring Cloud Stream?

Event-driven architecture (EDA) is an architectural pattern that involves the production, detection, consumption, and reaction to events that occur within a system. Spring Cloud Stream is a framework that allows developers to build event-driven microservices that communicate via messaging systems.

To implement event-driven architecture in a Spring application using Spring Cloud Stream, you can follow these steps:

1. Define the Event Models - You have to define the events that will be produced and consumed within the system. Each event should have a unique identifier, and should contain enough information for the consumers to act upon it.

```
public class UserCreatedEvent {
    private Long id;
    private String name;
    private String email;

    // getters and setters
}
```

2. Binders Configuration - Binders provide the connectivity for your application by connecting the input and output channels of your Spring Cloud Stream application to the messaging system youre using.

```
spring.cloud.stream.binders.<your-binder-name>.type=<your-binder-
    type>
spring.cloud.stream.binders.<your-binder-name>.environment.<your-
    binder-property>=<your-binder-value>
```

3. Producer - Create producer that publishes events on the topic or channel. This is where Spring Cloud Stream comes into play, with annotations such as @EnableBinding and @Stream-Listener, allowing your application to produce and consume messages from the configured binder.

```
@EnableBinding(Source.class)
public class UserCreatedEventProducer {
    private final Source source;

    public UserCreatedEventProducer(Source source) {
        this.source = source;
    }

    public void publishUserCreatedEvent(UserCreatedEvent
        userCreatedEvent) {
        source.output().send(MessageBuilder.withPayload(
```

```
            userCreatedEvent).build());
    }
}
```

4. Consumer - Create consumer that subscribes to the topic or channel.

```
@EnableBinding(Sink.class)
public class UserCreatedEventConsumer {
    @StreamListener(Sink.INPUT)
    public void onUserCreated(UserCreatedEvent userCreatedEvent) {
        // Do something with the event
    }
}
```

5. Run Application - Run this application or deploy it to your server. Once you publish any event by calling 'publishUser-CreatedEvent' method, it will be consumed by the subscribed consumers.

Spring Cloud Stream adds an abstraction layer that allows developers to decouple their microservices from the underlying messaging technology. This makes it easy to change or upgrade the messaging system in the future without changing the application code.

5.16   Explain the role of Spring Cloud Sleuth and Zipkin in distributed tracing for microservices applications.

Spring Cloud Sleuth and Zipkin are two powerful tools that are used for distributed tracing in microservices applications.

Distributed tracing is a technique used to understand how microservices interact with each other in a complex microservices architecture, by tracing a request through multiple microservices. Essentially, distributed tracing allows developers to identify bottlenecks, troubleshoot issues and optimize performance in a microservices environment.

Spring Cloud Sleuth is a Spring Cloud component that provides distributed tracing capabilities for microservices. It generates trace and span ids for a request, which can be used to trace a request as it moves through multiple microservices. It also adds relevant tracing information to log statements, which makes troubleshooting issues easier. This way, Spring Cloud Sleuth helps to increase transparency and observability in a microservices architecture.

Zipkin is an open-source distributed tracing system that collects and analyzes traces from microservices. It provides a user interface to visualize the trace data, allowing developers to easily track requests as they move through the different microservices in the architecture.

With Zipkin and Spring Cloud Sleuth, a developer can:

- Trace a request through multiple microservices and identify any bottlenecks

- Analyze slow requests and optimize performance

- Debug and troubleshoot issues by identifying which microservices are causing an issue

- Monitor application behavior and understand how microservices are interacting with each other

To implement distributed tracing with Spring Cloud Sleuth and Zipkin, the first step is to include the respective dependencies in your microservices project. Then, you can configure them by adding relevant properties in the 'application.properties' or 'application.yml' file. After enabling distributed tracing, you can access the Zipkin dashboard to visualize and analyze the request traces.

Here's an example configuration in 'application.yml' for using Zipkin with Spring Cloud Sleuth:

```
spring:
  application:
    name: example-service

  sleuth:
    sampler:
      probability: 1.0

  zipkin:
    base-url: http://zipkinserver:9411
```

In this configuration, 'spring.sleuth' enables distributed tracing with a probability of 1.0, meaning that every request will be traced. 'spring.zipkin' is used to specify the URL for the Zipkin server.

Overall, Spring Cloud Sleuth and Zipkin provide a powerful mechanism for distributed tracing and help to increase observability and transparency in a microservices architecture.

5.17 What is Spring Cloud Kubernetes, and how does it help in deploying and managing Spring Boot applications on Kubernetes?

Spring Cloud Kubernetes is a framework that provides integration between the Spring Boot applications and the Kubernetes platform. It helps developers to leverage the benefits of Kubernetes, such as scalability, fault tolerance, and self-healing capabilities, while still utilizing the simplicity and productivity of Spring Boot.

One of the main advantages of using Spring Cloud Kubernetes is the simplification of the deployment process. Developers can package their Spring Boot applications as container images and deploy them to Kubernetes clusters using Kubernetes manifests. Spring Cloud Kubernetes helps in creating the manifests by providing annotations that map the Spring Boot components to Kubernetes objects. For example, the '@Service' annotation can be used to create a Kubernetes service for a Spring Boot application.

Another benefit of Spring Cloud Kubernetes is the discovery and registration of services. Kubernetes provides a built-in service discovery mechanism, but it requires configuring and managing multiple components. Spring Cloud Kubernetes simplifies this process by providing an integration with Spring Cloud Discovery, allowing developers to register their Spring Boot services and have them discovered by the other services in the cluster.

In addition to deployment and discovery, Spring Cloud Kubernetes also provides support for configurations and secrets. It allows developers to inject Kubernetes ConfigMaps and Secrets as Spring properties, making it easy to manage the configuration of the Spring Boot applications without changing the code.

To summarize, Spring Cloud Kubernetes is a framework that allows developers to seamlessly deploy and manage Spring Boot applications on Kubernetes. It provides integration for deployment, discovery, configurations, and secrets, simplifying the development process and allowing developers to focus on the business logic of their applications.

5.18 How can you use Project Reactor and Spring WebFlux for creating non-blocking, reactive applications in Spring?

Project Reactor is a reactive programming library designed specifically for the Java virtual machine, and it provides a set of building blocks for creating reactive applications. Spring WebFlux is a web framework that is built on top of Project Reactor and is designed specifically for creating reactive web applications in the Spring ecosystem.

Using Project Reactor and Spring WebFlux, we can create non-blocking, reactive applications in Spring. Here are the steps we can follow to create such applications:

1. Add the necessary dependencies To use Project Reactor and Spring WebFlux in our Spring application, we need to add the following dependencies to our project:

```
<dependency>
    <groupId>org.springframework.boot</groupId>
    <artifactId>spring-boot-starter-webflux</artifactId>
</dependency>

<dependency>
    <groupId>io.projectreactor</groupId>
    <artifactId>reactor-core</artifactId>
</dependency>
```

2. Create a reactive MongoDB repository To create a reactive MongoDB repository in Spring, we need to extend the ReactiveMongoRepository interface provided by Spring Data MongoDB. Here is an example:

```
import org.springframework.data.mongodb.repository.
   ReactiveMongoRepository;

public interface PersonRepository extends ReactiveMongoRepository<
   Person, String> {

}
```

3. Create a reactive controller To create a reactive controller
in Spring WebFlux, we need to annotate our controller methods with the @GetMapping, @PostMapping, @PutMapping, or
@DeleteMapping annotations. Here is an example:

```
import org.springframework.web.bind.annotation.GetMapping;
import org.springframework.web.bind.annotation.RestController;
import reactor.core.publisher.Flux;

@RestController
public class PersonController {

    private final PersonRepository personRepository;

    public PersonController(PersonRepository personRepository) {
        this.personRepository = personRepository;
    }

    @GetMapping("/persons")
    public Flux<Person> getAllPersons() {
       return personRepository.findAll();
    }

}
```

4. Use reactive streams To use reactive streams in our application, we can use the following Project Reactor types: Flux,
Mono, and FluxSink. Here is an example:

```
import reactor.core.publisher.Flux;
import reactor.core.publisher.Mono;

public class PersonService {

    private final PersonRepository personRepository;

    public PersonService(PersonRepository personRepository) {
        this.personRepository = personRepository;
    }

    public Flux<Person> getAllPersons() {
       return personRepository.findAll();
```

```
    }

    public Mono<Person> getPersonById(String id) {
        return personRepository.findById(id);
    }

    public Flux<Person> getPersonsByName(String name) {
        return personRepository.findByName(name);
    }

    public Mono<Person> savePerson(Person person) {
        return personRepository.save(person);
    }

}
```

In summary, we can use Project Reactor and Spring WebFlux to create non-blocking, reactive applications in Spring by adding the necessary dependencies, creating a reactive MongoDB repository, creating a reactive controller, and using reactive streams.

5.19 Explain the role of Spring Data's Querydsl support in creating type-safe, dynamic queries for database operations.

Spring Data Querydsl is a powerful feature of the Spring framework that provides support for creating type-safe dynamic database queries using Querydsl, a popular query language in the Java ecosystem. In traditional applications, developers write SQL queries by hand, which are error-prone and often lack type safety. Querydsl, on the other hand, allows developers to write SQL-like queries in Java code, which are then translated into SQL syntax at runtime.

Spring Data Querydsl leverages this feature by providing a set of abstractions that make it easy to integrate Querydsl queries into Spring Data repositories. Developers can use Querydsl predicates to create dynamic queries that can be executed against various database backends. This allows developers to build robust, type-safe, and flexible queries without worrying about the underlying syntax of their chosen database.

Spring Data Querydsl provides a number of features that make it a powerful tool for creating type-safe, dynamic queries:

1. Type safety: With Querydsl, developers can write queries in a type-safe manner. Spring Data Querydsl takes this a step further, providing additional type safety through interfaces and Java generics.

2. Dynamic queries: Querydsl predicates provide a flexible and powerful way to create dynamic queries that can be executed against various database backends.

3. Integration with Spring Data repositories: Spring Data Querydsl integrates seamlessly with Spring Data repositories, allowing developers to use Querydsl queries across various database backends.

4. Code generation: Querydsl has code generation tools that simplify the creation of query expressions.

5. Support for multiple backends: Spring Data Querydsl can work with a variety of databases, including relational databases and NoSQL databases like MongoDB.

To illustrate the use of Querydsl with Spring Data, consider the following example:

```
QUser user = QUser.user;
```

```
Predicate predicate = user.firstName.eq("John").and(user.lastName.
    containsIgnoreCase("doe"));
List<User> users = userRepository.findAll(predicate);
```

In this example, we use Querydsl to create a type-safe predicate that finds all users whose first name is "John" and last name contains "doe" (case-insensitive). We then use this predicate to find all matching users using the 'findAll' method of the repository.

Overall, Spring Data Querydsl is a powerful tool for creating type-safe, dynamic queries in Spring applications. It provides a flexible and powerful way to build queries that can be executed against various database backends, making it an essential tool for modern application development.

5.20   How can you optimize performance in a Spring application using various profiling and monitoring tools?

Optimizing performance in a Spring application requires a thorough understanding of the application's architecture, performance bottlenecks, and the tools available for profiling and monitoring. Here are some ways to optimize performance in a Spring application:

1. Use a profiler: Profiling tools help in identifying performance bottlenecks in the application. Some popular profilers are VisualVM, YourKit, and JProfiler. Profilers can help in identifying hotspots in the application code, memory leaks, and excessive object creation.

2. Use caching: Caching helps in reducing the number of requests to the database and can improve the application's response time. Spring provides various caching mechanisms like '@Cacheable', '@CachePut', and '@CacheEvict'. These annotations can be used to cache the results of expensive methods, reducing the computational load.

3. Use a load testing tool: A load testing tool can simulate heavy traffic to the application and help in identifying performance bottlenecks. Popular load testing tools include Apache JMeter and Gatling.

4. Use APM tools: Application Performance Monitoring (APM) tools track application metrics like CPU usage, memory usage, and response time. Spring applications can be monitored using tools like New Relic, AppDynamics, and Dynatrace.

5. Use connection pooling: Connection pooling can improve the performance of database connections. Spring provides support for popular connection pooling libraries like HikariCP and Tomcat Connection Pool.

6. Optimize database queries: Database queries can be optimized for better performance. Tools like Hibernate's 'show_sql' property and the Spring datasource's 'log_statement' property can be used to monitor database queries and identify slow queries.

In summary, optimizing performance in a Spring application requires using various tools and techniques like profiling, caching, load testing, APM, connection pooling, and database query optimization. These tools and techniques can help in identifying and resolving performance bottlenecks, improving the application's response time, and enhancing the end-user experience.

Chapter 6

Guru

6.1 How can you design and implement a custom namespace handler and schema for Spring XML configuration?

In Spring Framework's XML configuration, custom namespaces are an essential concept that allows application developers to extend the default set of XML tags and attributes. These custom namespaces improve modularity and make it easier to manage the configuration of complex applications. Creating custom namespace handlers and schemas enables developers to define their own XML elements and attributes within their modules while complying with the prescribed syntax and semantics of Spring's Configuration schema.

A namespace handler is used to register the custom XML tag to the Spring Context namespace. The Spring Context namespace is used to define Spring beans, their dependencies, and various configuration settings. In contrast, a custom schema is used to define the syntax of the XML tag, including its attributes and child elements, that are used by a custom namespace.

Here is an overview of the steps required to design and implement a custom namespace handler and schema in Spring:

Step 1: Load the Schema

The first step is to define the custom schema itself. The XML schema file must be loaded via the Spring 'Resource' interface. Here is an example using the 'ClassPathResource' implementation:

```
public class MyNamespaceHandler extends NamespaceHandlerSupport {
    public void init() {
        Resource schemaLocation = new ClassPathResource("my/schema.
            xsd");

        registerBeanDefinitionParser("myelement", new
            MyBeanDefinitionParser(schemaLocation));
    }
}
```

Step 2: Define the Namespace Handler

The next step is to define the namespace handler. The handler is responsible for parsing the XML and delegating the processing to the appropriate parser. Here is an example of a 'NamespaceHandler' implementation:

```
public class MyNamespaceHandler extends NamespaceHandlerSupport {
    public void init() {
        registerBeanDefinitionParser("myelement", new
            MyBeanDefinitionParser());
    }
}
```

Step 3: Define the Bean Definition Parser

The 'BeanDefinitionParser' interface is responsible for parsing the custom XML element and returning a 'BeanDefinition'. Here is an example of a 'BeanDefinitionParser' implementation:

```
public class MyBeanDefinitionParser extends
    AbstractBeanDefinitionParser {
  protected AbstractBeanDefinition parseInternal(Element element,
      ParserContext parserContext) {
    BeanDefinitionBuilder builder = BeanDefinitionBuilder.
        rootBeanDefinition(MyClass.class);
    String attributeValue = element.getAttribute("myattribute");
    builder.addPropertyValue("myProperty", attributeValue);
    return builder.getBeanDefinition();
  }
}
```

This example creates an instance of the 'MyClass' bean and sets its 'myProperty' property to the value of the 'myattribute' attribute in the XML element.

Step 4: Declare the Custom Namespace

Lastly, the custom namespace must be declared in the application context XML file. This is done by adding an 'xmlns' attribute to the root element of the XML file for the custom namespace.

```
<beans xmlns="http://www.springframework.org/schema/beans
       xmlns:xsi="http://www.w3.org/2001/XMLSchema-instance
       xmlns:my="http://www.example.com/schema/my"
       xsi:schemaLocation="http://www.springframework.org/schema/
           beans http://www.springframework.org/schema/beans/spring-
           beans.xsd
           http://www.example.com/schema/my http://www.example.com/
           schema/my.xsd">

    <my:myelement myattribute="myvalue"/>

</beans>
```

In this example, the 'my' namespace is registered to the 'http://www.example.com/schema/my' URL, and the 'myelement' element, which is defined in the 'my.xsd' schema file, can now be used in the XML configuration.

In conclusion, designing and implementing a custom namespace
handler and schema requires a few essential steps. Implementing these steps correctly will enable you to define and use custom XML elements and attributes in the Spring configuration
file, while providing better modularity and manageability to the
application.

6.2   Explain the concept of bean defini-tion inheritance and how it can be used for modularizing Spring config-urations.

Bean definition inheritance is a powerful feature of Spring Framework that allows developers to define a hierarchy of bean definitions in which child beans inherit configurations from their
parent beans. It's a convenient way to reduce code duplication
and achieve modularity in Spring configurations.

To understand how bean definition inheritance works, let's take
an example of a simple Spring configuration. Assume we have
two beans, 'dataSource' and 'transactionManager'.

```
<bean id="dataSource" class="com.example.DataSource">
  <property name="url" value="jdbc:mysql://localhost/test"/>
  <property name="username" value="root"/>
  <property name="password" value=""/>
</bean>

<bean id="transactionManager" class="org.springframework.jdbc.
    datasource.DataSourceTransactionManager">
  <property name="dataSource" ref="dataSource"/>
</bean>
```

Here the 'dataSource' bean defines the connection parameters and the 'transactionManager' bean depends on 'dataSource' for transaction management.

Now suppose we have more than one data source with the same configuration except for the URL. In this case, we can use bean definition inheritance to avoid duplicating the 'dataSource' configuration. We can define a parent 'dataSource' bean and sub-beans can inherit the configuration and override the URL property.

```
<bean id="parentDataSource" abstract="true" class="com.example.
    DataSource">
  <property name="username" value="root"/>
  <property name="password" value=""/>
</bean>

<bean id="dataSource1" parent="parentDataSource">
  <property name="url" value="jdbc:mysql://localhost/test1"/>
</bean>

<bean id="dataSource2" parent="parentDataSource">
  <property name="url" value="jdbc:mysql://localhost/test2"/>
</bean>

<bean id="transactionManager" class="org.springframework.jdbc.
    datasource.DataSourceTransactionManager">
  <property name="dataSource" ref="dataSource1"/>
</bean>
```

Here the 'parentDataSource' bean is defined with the common configuration options, and the sub-beans 'dataSource1' and 'dataSource2' override only the 'url' property. The 'abstract="true"' attribute in the 'parentDataSource' bean definition indicates that it is a template bean and cannot be instantiated directly.

Note that bean definition inheritance can be used not only for data source configurations but also for any other type of bean definitions. It's a powerful way of building modular and reusable Spring configurations.

6.3   How can you implement advanced method-level security using Spring Security's Pre and Post annotations with SpEL expressions?

Spring Security's Pre and Post annotations provide powerful method-level security mechanisms. These annotations are used to enforce access control rules on specific methods in your application code.

To implement advanced method-level security using Pre and Post annotations with SpEL (Spring Expression Language) expressions, follow these steps:

1. Add the Spring Security dependency to your project's build file.

2. Configure Spring Security by defining a security configuration class that extends WebSecurityConfigurerAdapter. In this class, you can configure method-level security by using the @EnableGlobalMethodSecurity annotation.

For example, the following code snippet enables method-level security with pre- and post-invocation checks:

```
@Configuration
@EnableGlobalMethodSecurity(prePostEnabled=true)
public class MethodSecurityConfig extends
    WebSecurityConfigurerAdapter {
    @Override
    protected void configure(HttpSecurity http) throws Exception {
        // configure HTTP security
    }
}
```

3. Define access control rules for specific methods using Pre

and Post annotations. You can use SpEL expressions in these annotations to specify the conditions under which a method can be invoked.

For example, the following code snippet shows a method-level security rule that allows only authenticated users with the ROLE_AD-MIN authority to invoke the method:

```
@PreAuthorize("hasRole('ROLE_ADMIN')␣and␣isAuthenticated()")
public void someSecureMethod() {
    // method implementation
}
```

4. Use the Spring Expression Language (SpEL) to define more complex conditions that involve method arguments or return values. For example, you can use SpEL to validate method arguments or to restrict method invocation based on the value of a specific property.

For example, the following code snippet shows how to use SpEL to validate the argument of a method:

```
@PreAuthorize("#param␣!=␣null␣and␣#param.length()␣>␣0")
public void secureMethod(String param) {
    // method implementation
}
```

In this example, the method is allowed to execute only when the 'param' variable is not null and has a length greater than 0.

Overall, Spring Security's Pre and Post annotations with SpEL expressions provide a flexible and powerful method-level security mechanism that allows you to enforce access control rules on specific methods in your application.

6.4   Explain how Spring supports transaction isolation levels and how to configure them in your application.

Spring supports various transaction isolation levels. Transaction isolation levels are defined by the ACID (Atomicity, Consistency, Isolation, and Durability) properties of the database transactions.

Isolation levels define the degree of isolation among transactions that are executing concurrently in a database. The levels determine the maximum degree of interference that transactions are allowed to have with each other. Lower levels provide higher concurrency but lower data integrity, while higher levels provide better data integrity but lower concurrency.

Spring supports the following five transaction isolation levels:

1. READ_UNCOMMITTED

2. READ_COMMITTED

3. REPEATABLE_READ

4. SERIALIZABLE

5. DEFAULT

You can configure the transaction isolation levels for Spring transactions either programmatically or declaratively.

Programmatic configuration involves setting the transaction isolation level for the transaction using the TransactionTemplate class or the Transactional annotation.

Here's an example of programmatic configuration using the 'TransactionTemplate' class:

```
TransactionTemplate transactionTemplate = new TransactionTemplate(
    transactionManager);
transactionTemplate.setIsolationLevel(TransactionDefinition.
    ISOLATION_SERIALIZABLE);
transactionTemplate.execute(new TransactionCallbackWithoutResult() {
    protected void doInTransactionWithoutResult(TransactionStatus
        status) {
      // your transactional logic here
    }
});
```

Declarative configuration involves declaring the transaction isolation level in the Spring configuration file using the 'tx:annotation-driven' element and the '@Transactional' annotation.

Here's an example of declarative configuration:

```
<!-- Configure transaction manager -->
<bean id="txnManager" class="org.springframework.jdbc.datasource.
    DataSourceTransactionManager">
  <property name="dataSource" ref="dataSource"/>
</bean>

<!-- Enable transaction annotations -->
<tx:annotation-driven transaction-manager="txnManager"/>

<!-- Define a service bean -->
<bean id="userService" class="com.example.UserService"/>

<!-- Declare transactional methods -->
<tx:advice id="txAdvice" transaction-manager="txnManager">
  <tx:attributes>
    <tx:method name="add*" isolation="SERIALIZABLE" propagation="
        REQUIRED" rollback-for="Exception"/>
    <tx:method name="update*" isolation="READ_COMMITTED"
        propagation="REQUIRED" rollback-for="Exception"/>
    <tx:method name="delete*" isolation="READ_COMMITTED"
        propagation="REQUIRED" rollback-for="Exception"/>
    <tx:method name="get*" isolation="READ_UNCOMMITTED" read-only
        ="true"/>
  </tx:attributes>
</tx:advice>

<aop:config>
  <aop:pointcut id="userServicePointcut" expression="execution(*
      com.example.UserService.*(..))"/>
  <aop:advisor pointcut-ref="userServicePointcut" advice-ref="
      txAdvice"/>
</aop:config>
```

In this example, the 'add*' method uses the 'SERIALIZABLE'
isolation level, 'update*' and 'delete*' methods use the 'READ_COM-
MITTED' isolation level, and 'get*' methods use the 'READ_UN-
COMMITTED' isolation level.

In summary, Spring supports various transaction isolation levels, and you can configure them either programmatically or
declaratively using the 'TransactionTemplate' class or the '@Trans-
actional' annotation in conjunction with the 'tx:annotation-
driven' element in the Spring configuration file.

6.5   How can you implement advanced performance optimizations in Spring JDBC, such as batching, fetch size, and pagination?

Spring provides multiple ways to implement advanced performance optimizations in Spring JDBC. Let's discuss each of
them below -

1. Batching - Batching is the process of sending multiple SQL
statements as a single request to the database server. This
reduces network round trips and improves performance. Spring
JDBC provides support for batch updates using JdbcTemplate
class. You can batch updates as below -

```
jdbcTemplate.batchUpdate("INSERT INTO Employee(name, age) VALUES (?,
    ?)", new BatchPreparedStatementSetter() {

    @Override
    public void setValues(PreparedStatement ps, int i) throws
        SQLException {
        ps.setString(1, employees.get(i).getName());
        ps.setInt(2, employees.get(i).getAge());
```

```
    }
    @Override
    public int getBatchSize() {
        return employees.size();
    }
});
```

2. Fetch Size - Fetch Size is the number of rows fetched from the database at a time. By default, JDBC fetches all the rows at once, but this can cause performance issues if the table has a large number of rows. Spring JDBC provides a way to set the fetch size using the StatementCreatorUtils class as below -

```
jdbcTemplate.query("SELECT * FROM Employee", new RowMapper<Employee
    >() {
    @Override
    public Employee mapRow(ResultSet rs, int rowNum) throws
        SQLException {
        // ...
    }
}, stmt -> {
    stmt.setFetchSize(50);
});
```

3. Pagination - Pagination is the process of retrieving a subset of results from a large dataset. Spring JDBC provides pagination support using the JdbcTemplate class. You can use 'LIMIT' or 'OFFSET' clauses to retrieve a specific subset of results. The 'LIMIT' and 'OFFSET' clauses can be added to your SQL query as below -

```
int pageSize = 10;
int pageNumber = 2;
int offset = (pageNumber - 1) * pageSize;

String sql = "SELECT * FROM Employee LIMIT ? OFFSET ?";
List<Employee> employees = jdbcTemplate.query(sql, new
    EmployeeMapper(), pageSize, offset);
```

In the above code, the 'pageSize' determines how many records should be returned per page, while 'pageNumber' determines which page to return.

In conclusion, Spring JDBC provides several ways to optimize performance, and batching, fetch size, and pagination are some of the techniques you can use to improve performance while working with large datasets. By optimizing the performance, you can reduce the application's response time and improve the user experience.

6.6 What are the strategies for handling deadlocks and lock timeouts in Spring transaction management?

Deadlocks and lock timeouts can occur when multiple transactions are trying to access the same resource at the same time. This can cause the transactions to wait indefinitely for each other to release the resource, resulting in a deadlock. To handle deadlocks and lock timeouts in Spring transaction management, there are several strategies that can be employed.

1. Optimistic locking: One strategy for avoiding the occurrence of deadlocks and lock timeouts in Spring transaction management is to use optimistic locking. This strategy involves the creation of a version field for each entity that controls concurrency. This version field is checked before updates are made to ensure that the data has not been modified by another transaction. If the data has been modified, the transaction is rolled back, and an exception is thrown.

Example:

```
@Entity
```

```
public class Employee {

    @Id
    @GeneratedValue(strategy = GenerationType.IDENTITY)
    private Long id;

    private String name;

    @Version
    private Long version;

    // setters and getters
}
```

2. Pessimistic locking: Another strategy for handling deadlocks and lock timeouts in Spring transaction management is to use pessimistic locking. This strategy involves acquiring locks on the resources before performing any updates. This approach ensures that no other transaction can change the resource while it is locked.

Example:

```
@Lock(LockModeType.PESSIMISTIC_WRITE)
public Employee updateEmployee(Long employeeId) {
    Employee employee = entityManager.find(Employee.class,
        employeeId);
    // code to modify employee object
    entityManager.flush();
    return employee;
}
```

3. Timeout settings: Spring transaction management allows the configuration of timeout settings for transactions. This configuration provides a maximum time limit for a transaction to complete its execution. If the transaction exceeds the specified time limit, it is rolled back, and an exception is thrown. This strategy ensures that transactions do not wait indefinitely for resources.

Example:

```
@Transactional(timeout = 5)
public void updateEmployeeSalary(Long employeeId, double salary) {
    Employee employee = entityManager.find(Employee.class,
        employeeId);
    // code to update salary
}
```

4. Retry mechanism: Spring transaction management allows the configuration of a retry mechanism for transactions. This configuration provides a maximum number of attempts for a transaction to complete its execution. If the transaction fails, it is retried after a specified time interval. This strategy ensures that transactions are retried, even if they encounter deadlocks.

Example:

```
@Bean
public SpringRetryConfiguration springRetryConfiguration() {
    return new SpringRetryConfiguration()
                .setDefaultRetryAttempts(3)
                .setDefaultBackOffPolicy("fixedDelay", 5000);
}

@Retryable
@Override
@Transactional
public void performTransaction() {
    // code to perform transaction
}
```

In conclusion, handling deadlocks and lock timeouts in Spring transaction management requires the use of different strategies. Employing any of the above strategies will help ensure that transactions are completed without incurring an indefinite wait time, thus improving system performance and data consistency.

6.7 Discuss the internals of Spring AOP and how it creates proxy objects for implementing cross-cutting concerns.

Spring AOP (Aspect-Oriented Programming) is a powerful tool that allows developers to implement cross-cutting concerns in their applications without having to modify the source code of the application classes directly. The main concept behind Spring AOP is to use a combination of Aspect and Advices to implement cross-cutting concerns in the application without modifying its core logic. In this answer, we'll discuss the internals of Spring AOP and how it creates proxy objects for implementing cross-cutting concerns.

When a Spring AOP-based application is executed, Spring creates proxy objects for the application's classes. These proxy objects are used to apply cross-cutting concerns to the application, while leaving the original application classes untouched. The proxy objects are created based on the configured AOP aspects and advice.

Internally, Spring uses a special proxy object known as a "dynamic proxy" to implement the AOP features. Dynamic proxies are created at runtime by implementing the interfaces of the classes that they're proxying. The dynamic proxy intercepts method calls on the class it's proxying and delegates those calls to the appropriate advice classes based on the pointcut configured in the AOP aspect.

There are two types of proxies that Spring AOP uses - JDK Dynamic Proxies and CGLIB proxies.

JDK Dynamic Proxies are used when the target class being

proxied implements one or more interfaces. In JDK Dynamic
Proxy-based AOP, Spring creates a proxy object that implements the interfaces of the target class and then delegates the
method calls to the appropriate advice classes based on the
pointcut configured in the AOP aspect.

CGLIB proxies are used when the target class being proxied
does not implement any interfaces. In CGLIB Proxy-based
AOP, Spring creates a subclass of the target class and then delegates the method calls to the appropriate advice classes based
on the pointcut configured in the AOP aspect.

To summarize, Spring AOP uses proxy objects to implement
cross-cutting concerns in an application. These proxies are created at runtime using either JDK Dynamic Proxy or CGLIB
Proxy. The dynamic proxy intercepts method calls on the class
it's proxying and delegates those calls to the appropriate advice
classes based on the pointcut configured in the AOP aspect.
This allows developers to add cross-cutting concerns to their
applications without having to modify the original application
classes.

6.8   How can you use Spring Boot's cus-
tom auto-configuration and starter modules to create reusable components for
your applications?

Spring Boot's custom auto-configuration and starter modules
allow developers to create reusable components for their applications in a seamless manner.

Custom auto-configuration is a feature in Spring Boot that enables developers to automatically configure third-party libraries to integrate with their application. This feature eliminates the need for developers to manually configure dependencies, as Spring Boot automatically configures the dependencies based on the classpath.

Custom starter modules, on the other hand, are a set of preconfigured dependencies that can be bundled into a single, reusable module. These modules can be used to quickly configure and bootstrap an application with the necessary dependencies, without having to manually include and configure each dependency.

Here are some steps to create a custom auto-configuration and starter module in Spring Boot:

1. Identify the libraries or dependencies that your application needs to function properly. For instance, let's say you need to configure a database connection, a message broker, and a logging framework.

2. Create an auto-configuration class for each dependency. The auto-configuration classes should implement the 'org.springframework.boot.autoconfigure.condition.ConditionalOnClass' annotation, enabling Spring Boot to only configure the dependencies if the corresponding class is present.

For example, let's say you want to configure a database connection using the Hikari connection pool. You can create an auto-configuration class as follows:

```
@Configuration
@ConditionalOnClass(HikariDataSource.class)
public class DatabaseAutoConfiguration {
    @Bean
    @ConfigurationProperties("spring.datasource.hikari")
    public DataSource dataSource() {
```

```
        return new HikariDataSource();
    }
}
```

This auto-configuration class will only configure the database if 'HikariDataSource' is present in the application classpath.

3. Bundle the auto-configuration classes into a starter module. To do this, create a new Maven or Gradle project and add the auto-configuration classes as dependencies. You can also add any other libraries or dependencies that your application requires.

4. Publish the starter module to a repository. Once the starter module is published, it can be easily included in other applications by including its dependency in the application's build configuration file.

With these steps, developers can easily create reusable components for their applications using Spring Boot's custom auto-configuration and starter modules. These components can be included and configured in any Spring Boot application with minimum effort.

6.9   What are the strategies for handling large data sets and optimizing performance in Spring Batch applications?

Spring Batch is a powerful framework for processing large data sets in batch jobs. However, with large volumes of data, performance can become a concern. In this context, there are a number of strategies that can be used to optimize the performance of Spring Batch applications.

1. Partitioning: Partitioning refers to splitting a large job into smaller, independently executable sub-jobs. Spring Batch supports several partitioning strategies, including range-based partitioning and random partitioning. The main advantage of partitioning is that it allows for parallel processing of sub-jobs, which can significantly reduce processing time.

2. Chunk-oriented Processing: Chunk-oriented processing is a key feature of Spring Batch that allows for efficient processing of large data sets. Essentially, a chunk refers to a subset of data that can be processed together in a single transaction. By processing data in chunks, rather than one record at a time, the overhead of transaction management and database access is reduced, which can improve performance.

3. Paging and Sorting: Spring Batch provides built-in support for paging and sorting data, which is particularly useful for working with large datasets. By paginating, we minimize the amount of data loaded into memory at one time, which reduces memory pressure and improves performance. Similarly, sorting data can be an effective strategy for optimizing database queries, and Spring Batch provides robust support for sorting data in both in-memory and database-backed scenarios.

4. Caching: Caching refers to storing frequently accessed data in memory, rather than repeatedly querying the database. This can help improve the performance of Spring Batch applications by reducing the amount of network traffic and database load. Spring provides a number of caching solutions, such as Ehcache, that can help optimize performance.

5. Threading: Threading refers to the use of multiple threads of

execution to perform different tasks simultaneously. In Spring Batch, this can be used to speed up the execution of a job, by performing multiple processing steps in parallel. Spring Batch provides support for multithreaded processing through the use of task-execution frameworks such as ThreadPoolTaskExecutor.

6. Use of JPA: If you're working with a large amount of data, you should consider using a JPA (Java Persistence API) implementation like Hibernate, because JPA provides a lot of convenience methods and a large number of caching options. Hibernate, Springs JPA provider, has built-in query caching and second-level caching that can improve database performance considerably.

In conclusion, there are several strategies for handling large data sets and optimizing performance in Spring Batch applications. By employing these strategies, you can build more efficient and scalable batch processing systems that can handle high-volume data processing with ease.

6.10   Explain the architectural patterns and best practices for building microservices using Spring Boot and Spring Cloud.

When building microservices using Spring Boot and Spring Cloud, there are several architectural patterns and best practices that can be followed to ensure the reliability, scalability, and maintainability of the application. The following are some of the major architectural patterns and best practices that should be considered:

1. Microservices Architecture: The first and foremost architectural pattern for building microservices is to follow the principles of a microservices architecture. This means that each service should be developed as an independent and loosely coupled component, having its own business logic and data store. The communication between services should be done through lightweight protocols such as RESTful APIs, and each service should be developed and deployed independently.

2. Service Discovery: Another important architectural pattern is to implement service discovery, which helps in discovering and communicating with other microservices in the system. In Spring Cloud, this can be achieved using tools like Eureka or Consul, which provide a centralized registry of all the services in the system. Service discovery enables dynamic scaling of services, as new instances can be added to the system without affecting the availability of other services.

3. API Gateway: An API gateway is a key component in microservices architecture, as it provides a single entry point for all the API requests to the system. In Spring Cloud, this can be achieved using the Spring Cloud Gateway project, which provides a lightweight and scalable way to route requests to the relevant service. An API gateway also provides capabilities like authentication and rate limiting.

4. Circuit Breaker: A circuit breaker pattern is used to handle failures in microservices architecture. It prevents cascading failures in the system by isolating the services that are failing, and providing fallback options. In Spring Boot, this can be implemented using the Hystrix library, which provides circuit breaker functionality.

5. Distributed Tracing: Distributed tracing is an important best practice for microservices architecture, as it helps in monitoring the flow of requests through the system. In Spring Cloud, this can be implemented using tools like Zipkin, which provides visibility into the entire request tree and helps in identifying and troubleshooting issues.

6. Containerization: Another best practice for microservices architecture is to containerize each service using tools like Docker. This provides a lightweight and consistent environment for each service, which can be easily replicated and scaled.

7. Continuous Integration and Continuous Deployment (CI/CD): Finally, it is important to implement a robust CI/CD pipeline for the microservices application. This ensures that each service is built, tested, and deployed in a consistent and automated manner, which reduces the risk of errors and improves the overall quality of the application. In Spring Boot, this can be achieved using tools like Jenkins or GitLab CI/CD.

These are some of the major architectural patterns and best practices for building microservices using Spring Boot and Spring Cloud. By following these patterns and practices, developers can build highly scalable, resilient, and maintainable microservices applications.

6.11   How can you implement distributed caching and cache synchronization in a Spring application using Spring Cache and third-party caching solutions like Redis or Hazelcast?

Caching is essential to maintain the performance and scalability of any application. Distributed caching is a solution that stores the same data in multiple cache servers to achieve high availability, fault tolerance, and faster retrieval speed. In a Spring application, we can use Spring Cache along with third-party caching solutions like Redis, Hazelcast, or Ehcache to implement distributed caching and cache synchronization.

Here is a step-by-step guide to implementing distributed caching and cache synchronization using Spring Cache and Redis:

1. Add Redis dependency to your project:

```
<dependency>
    <groupId>org.springframework.boot</groupId>
    <artifactId>spring-boot-starter-data-redis</artifactId>
</dependency>
```

2. Configure Redis Cache Manager in your Spring configuration file. In this example, Redis is being used as the cache store:

```
@Bean
public RedisConnectionFactory redisConnectionFactory() {
    return new LettuceConnectionFactory(new
        RedisStandaloneConfiguration("localhost", 6379));
}

@Bean
public CacheManager cacheManager() {
    RedisCacheConfiguration redisCacheConfiguration =
        RedisCacheConfiguration.defaultCacheConfig()
        .entryTtl(Duration.ofMinutes(1))
```

```
                   .disableCachingNullValues();

        return RedisCacheManager.builder(redisConnectionFactory())
            .cacheDefaults(redisCacheConfiguration)
            .build();
    }
```

This configuration sets up the Redis server and creates the cache manager instance that is later used to interact with Redis.

3. Annotate methods that need to be cached with '@Cacheable'.

```
        @Cacheable(value = "exampleCache", key = "#id")
        public Example getCachedExample(String id) {
            return exampleService.getExample(id);
        }
```

This annotation tells Spring to use the 'CacheManager' to look up the cache named 'exampleCache'. When this method is called with 'id' parameter, Spring will try to fetch the cached result for the given 'id' from the cache. If it's a cache miss, then the method is executed, and the output is cached in Redis. Subsequent calls with the same 'id' get a cached result.

4. Refresh the cache when data is updated.

When data is updated, we need to refresh the cache to ensure that subsequent requests get the updated data. For that, we can use '@CachePut' annotation, which updates the cache with the new data.

```
        @CachePut(value = "exampleCache", key = "#id")
        public Example updateExample(String id, Example example) {
            return exampleService.updateExample(id, example);
        }
```

This method updates the 'example' object for the given 'id'. The updated object will be cached with the same 'id'. Subsequent calls with the same 'id' will get the updated data from the cache.

5. Remove data from the cache using '@CacheEvict' annotation

We might need to remove data from the cache when it is no longer needed or when it becomes stale. We can use the '@CacheEvict' annotation to remove data from the cache.

```
@CacheEvict(value = "exampleCache", key = "#id")
public void evictExample(String id) {
    exampleService.deleteExample(id);
}
```

This method deletes the 'example' object for the given 'id'. The cache entry with the same 'id' is removed from the cache.

6. Configure Hazelcast as a distributed cache store

Hazelcast is another popular distributed caching solution. We can use the 'spring-boot-starter-cache' dependency and 'hazelcast-spring' to use Hazelcast as a cache store.

```
<dependency>
    <groupId>com.hazelcast</groupId>
    <artifactId>hazelcast</artifactId>
</dependency>

<dependency>
    <groupId>com.hazelcast</groupId>
    <artifactId>hazelcast-spring</artifactId>
</dependency>

@Configuration
@EnableCaching
public class HazelcastConfig {

    @Bean
    public HazelcastInstance hazelcastInstance() {
        Config config = new Config();
        config.setInstanceName("hazelcast-instance")
            .addMapConfig(new MapConfig().setName("exampleCache
                ")
                .setMaxSizeConfig(new MaxSizeConfig(200,
                    MaxSizeConfig.MaxSizePolicy.
                    FREE_HEAP_SIZE))
```

```
                        .setEvictionPolicy(EvictionPolicy.LRU)
                        .setTimeToLiveSeconds(20));

        return Hazelcast.newHazelcastInstance(config);
    }

    @Bean
    public CacheManager cacheManager() {
        return new HazelcastCacheManager(hazelcastInstance());
    }
}
```

This configuration sets up the Hazelcast instance and creates the Hazelcast Cache manager instance that is later used to interact with Hazelcast.

In conclusion, distributed caching and cache synchronization are essential to maintain the performance and scalability of any application. In Spring, we can use Spring Cache along with third-party caching solutions like Redis or Hazelcast to implement distributed caching and cache synchronization. Implementing caching with Spring Cache and Redis is an easy way to start caching in your Spring application.

6.12 What are the strategies for implementing complex data access patterns, such as CQRS and Event Sourcing, using Spring Data and Spring Integration?

Implementing complex data access patterns such as CQRS (Command Query Responsibility Segregation) and Event Sourcing often involves a combination of different architectural patterns and technologies. In this answer, I will discuss how Spring

Data and Spring Integration can be used to implement CQRS
and Event Sourcing.

CQRS with Spring Data CQRS separates commands (write
operations) and queries (read operations) into different models,
which can be optimized for their specific tasks. In Spring Data,
this can be achieved by defining separate repositories for write
and read operations, with different query methods and entities.

For example, suppose we have an order management system
with a complex domain model. We can define a 'Comman-
dOrderRepository' for write operations, which exposes methods
for creating, updating, and deleting orders:

```
public interface CommandOrderRepository extends CrudRepository<Order
    , Long> {
  Order create(Order order);
  Order update(Order order);
  void delete(Long orderId);
}
```

We can also define a separate 'QueryOrderRepository' for read
operations, which exposes methods for querying orders based
on different criteria:

```
public interface QueryOrderRepository extends CrudRepository<
    OrderSummary, Long> {
  List<OrderSummary> findByCustomerId(Long customerId);
  List<OrderSummary> findByOrderStatus(OrderStatus status);
  List<OrderSummary> findByDateCreatedBetween(LocalDateTime
      startDate, LocalDateTime endDate);
}
```

By separating the read and write operations into different repositories, we can optimize each repository for its specific task, and
avoid performance issues caused by conflicting requirements.

Event Sourcing with Spring Integration Event Sourcing is a
pattern where we store every change to an entity as a sequenced

set of events. This allows us to rebuild the entire state of an
entity at any point in time, and also provides an audit trail
of all changes. Spring Integration can be used to implement
Event Sourcing by using message channels to store and retrieve
events.

For example, suppose we have a system that tracks the state of
an order. Instead of directly updating the order, we can define
a 'OrderEvent' entity to represent each change:

```
public class OrderEvent {
    private Long orderId;
    private LocalDateTime timestamp;
    private OrderStatus status;
    // ...
}
```

We can then use Spring Integration to store and retrieve these
events as messages on a message channel. Whenever a change
is made to the order, we store an event message on a 'orderEventChannel':

```
@MessagingGateway
public interface OrderEventGateway {
    @Gateway(requestChannel = "orderEventChannel")
    void send(OrderEvent event);
}

@Bean
public IntegrationFlow orderEventFlow() {
    return IntegrationFlows.from("orderEventChannel")
        .handle(/* store event in database */)
        .get();
}
```

To retrieve the state of an order at any point in time, we can
use a 'EventStore' class that queries the event messages on the
'orderEventChannel' and applies them in order:

```
public class OrderEventStore {
    public Order get(Long orderId) {
        List<OrderEvent> events = /* query database for events */
```

```
        Order order = new Order();
        for (OrderEvent e : events) {
            order.updateState(e);
        }
        return order;
    }
}
```

By using Spring Integration to store and retrieve events, we can implement Event Sourcing in a scalable and robust way, with support for distributed messaging and error handling.

Conclusion In summary, implementing complex data access patterns such as CQRS and Event Sourcing can be achieved using a combination of Spring Data and Spring Integration. By separating the read and write operations into different repositories and using message channels to store and retrieve events, we can optimize performance and provide robust support for these patterns.

6.13   How can you create custom Spring MVC view resolvers and view technologies for rendering non-standard response formats?

Spring MVC provides support for several view technologies such as JSP, Thymeleaf, Freemarker, etc. These view technologies are used to render the server-side templates into HTML responses that are sent to the client's browser. However, there may be situations where you need to create a custom view resolver to render non-standard response formats.

Here are the steps to create custom Spring MVC view resolvers and view technologies:

1. Extend the AbstractTemplateViewResolver class:

The AbstractTemplateViewResolver class is an abstract implementation of the ViewResolver interface. You can extend this class to create your custom view resolver. The AbstractTemplateViewResolver provides common functionality that is required by most view resolvers.

For example, you can create a custom view resolver for rendering JSON responses as follows:

```
public class JsonViewResolver extends AbstractTemplateViewResolver {

    public JsonViewResolver() {
        setViewClass(JsonView.class);
        setContentType("application/json");
    }
}
```

In this example, we have extended the AbstractTemplateViewResolver class and set the view class to be JsonView. We have also set the contentType to "application/json" so that the client knows that the response is in JSON format.

2. Implement the View interface:

The View interface provides the render() method that generates the response content. You need to create a class that implements this interface and provides the logic to generate the response content in the required format.

For example, you can create a JsonView as follows:

```
public class JsonView implements View {

    private List<String> modelKeys;
```

```
public JsonView(List<String> modelKeys) {
    this.modelKeys = modelKeys;
}

@Override
public String getContentType() {
    return "application/json";
}

@Override
public void render(Map<String, ?> model, HttpServletRequest
    request,
        HttpServletResponse response) throws Exception {
    ObjectMapper mapper = new ObjectMapper();
    Map<String, Object> result = new HashMap<>();
    for (String key : modelKeys) {
        Object value = model.get(key);
        if (value != null) {
            result.put(key, value);
        }
    }
    mapper.writeValue(response.getWriter(), result);
}
}
```

In this example, we have implemented the View interface and provided the logic to generate the JSON response. The Json-View takes a list of model keys that it will include in the response. We are using the Jackson ObjectMapper to serialize the response object into JSON and write it to the response output stream.

3. Register the custom view resolver:

Finally, you need to register your custom view resolver with Spring MVC. You can do this in your WebMvcConfigurerAdapter implementation as follows:

```
@Configuration
@EnableWebMvc
public class MyWebMvcConfig extends WebMvcConfigurerAdapter {

    @Override
    public void configureViewResolvers(ViewResolverRegistry registry
        ) {
        registry.viewResolver(new JsonViewResolver());
```

```
      }
   }
```

In this example, we have overridden the configureViewResolvers()
method of the WebMvcConfigurerAdapter and registered our
JsonViewResolver.

With these steps, you have created a custom view resolver and
a custom view technology to render non-standard response formats.

6.14   Discuss the internals of Spring WebFlux's reactive programming model and how it differs from traditional, imperative programming models.

The reactive programming model in Spring WebFlux is asynchronous and non-blocking, which is fundamentally different
from traditional, imperative programming models. In traditional programming, the code runs sequentially and blocks the
execution until a particular operation completes. In contrast,
reactive programming models allow for parallel processing of
multiple operations without waiting for the completion of one
operation before proceeding with the next.

Internally, Spring WebFlux uses the Reactor library to provide
a reactive programming model. Reactor is a reactive streams
implementation that allows developers to create asynchronous,
non-blocking code. It is based on four main components: the
Flux, Mono, Scheduler, and Processor.

- Flux: A Flux is an abstraction that represents a stream of data that can emit zero or more elements. It is a publisher that generates events and notifies subscribers when new events are available.

- Mono: A Mono is similar to a Flux, but it can only emit zero or one element. It is used for operations that produce a single result.

- Scheduler: A Scheduler is a thread pool used to schedule the execution of tasks. It manages the threads used for asynchronous operations and ensures that they are utilized efficiently.

- Processor: A Processor is a combination of a publisher and subscriber. It receives events from a publisher, processes them, and then publishes the results to subscribers.

Spring WebFlux uses these components to implement reactive programming. For example, when handling a request, Spring WebFlux returns a Flux or Mono object that represents the asynchronous operation. When the operation completes, the result is returned to the subscriber. This allows the application to continue processing other requests without being blocked by the operation.

Overall, the reactive programming model in Spring WebFlux provides better performance, scalability, and resource utilization compared to traditional, imperative programming models. However, it requires a different approach to development and may require a learning curve for developers who are not familiar with reactive programming.

6.15   Explain the role of backpressure in reactive programming and how it can be managed using Spring WebFlux and Project Reactor.

Backpressure refers to the ability of a reactive system to manage the flow of data between different components, ensuring that no component is overwhelmed by too much data. In other words, backpressure is a mechanism that allows reactive streams to handle situations where the rate of data production is faster than the rate of processing.

In a reactive system, backpressure is typically managed using the Reactive Streams specification, which defines a set of interfaces and protocols that describe how data should be exchanged between publishers and subscribers. The goal of these interfaces is to ensure that subscribers can only process data as quickly as they are able to, thus preventing the system from becoming overloaded.

Spring WebFlux and Project Reactor are two popular tools for building reactive systems in Java. In Spring WebFlux, backpressure is managed using the Reactor library, which provides a set of operators for handling backpressure in reactive streams.

One way to manage backpressure in Spring WebFlux is to use the 'onBackpressureBuffer()' operator, which allows you to buffer data when the downstream subscriber is not ready to receive it. For example, suppose you have a reactive stream that is publishing data at a high rate:

```
Flux.range(1, Integer.MAX_VALUE)
```

If you want to limit the rate of data consumption downstream, you can use the 'onBackpressureBuffer()' operator like this:

```
Flux.range(1, Integer.MAX_VALUE)
    .onBackpressureBuffer(10)
    .subscribe(System.out::println);
```

In this example, the 'onBackpressureBuffer()' operator specifies that data should be buffered if the downstream subscriber is not ready to receive it. The buffer size is set to 10, which means that up to 10 elements can be buffered before the upstream publisher blocks.

Another way to manage backpressure in Spring WebFlux is to use the 'sample()' or 'throttle()' operator, which allow you to control the rate of data production upstream. For example, suppose you have a publisher that is generating data at a high rate:

```
Flux.interval(Duration.ofMillis(100))
```

If you want to limit the rate of data production to once per second, you can use the 'sample()' operator like this:

```
Flux.interval(Duration.ofMillis(100))
    .sample(Duration.ofSeconds(1))
    .subscribe(System.out::println);
```

In this example, the 'sample()' operator specifies that only one element should be produced every second, regardless of how quickly the publisher is generating data.

Overall, backpressure is an important concept in reactive programming, and Spring WebFlux and Project Reactor provide a number of tools and operators for managing it effectively. By understanding how to use these tools and operators, you can build reactive systems that are efficient, scalable, and responsive to changing demands.

6.16   How can you implement advanced monitoring, logging, and tracing in a distributed Spring Boot and Spring Cloud application using open-source and commercial tools?

Effective monitoring, logging, and tracing are critical aspects of a distributed Spring Boot and Spring Cloud application as they help to identify issues and improve the performance of the application. To achieve advanced monitoring, logging, and tracing, we need to implement tools and frameworks in the application. Generally, we can implement these features using open-source or commercial tools.

Here are some of the ways to implement advanced monitoring, logging, and tracing in a distributed Spring Boot and Spring Cloud application using open-source and commercial tools:

1.   Metrics monitoring: We can use the open-source monitoring tool Prometheus to monitor the application's metrics. Prometheus can scrape data directly from a running Spring Boot application and store it in its time-series database for analysis and visualization using tools such as Grafana. We can also use commercial tools like AppDynamics, Dynatrace, and New Relic for monitoring Spring Boot applications.

2. Distributed tracing: We can use open-source tools like Zipkin and Jaeger for distributed tracing to monitor the microser-

vices communication flow. Spring Cloud Sleuth provides an easy way to integrate with these tools. Commercial tools like AppDynamics, Dynatrace, and New Relic also offer distributed tracing capabilities.

3. Logging: We can configure the application's loggers with tools such as Logback or Log4j2 to capture application logs. We can centralize the logs in tools like Graylog, ELK stack (Elasticsearch, Logstash, and Kibana), or Splunk for analysis and visualization. Commercial tools like Loggly and Papertrail can also be used for centralized logging.

4. Application Performance Monitoring (APM): Open-source APM tools like Pinpoint or Kamon can be used to monitor the performance of Spring Boot applications. These tools provide detailed insights into the application's performance and help in identifying performance bottlenecks. Commercial APM tools like AppDynamics, Dynatrace, and New Relic offer more advanced APM capabilities.

In summary, using open-source or commercial tools, we can implement advanced monitoring, logging, and tracing in a distributed Spring Boot and Spring Cloud application effectively. This enables us to understand the application's behavior in real-time and identify performance issues, helping us continuously improve the application's performance, and provide a better experience to end-users.

6.17   Discuss the challenges and best practices for migrating legacy monolithic applications to microservices architecture using Spring Boot and Spring Cloud.

Migrating legacy monolithic applications to microservices architecture can be a daunting task, but it can also bring significant benefits in terms of scalability, flexibility, and agility. The Spring Boot and Spring Cloud frameworks are popular choices for implementing microservices, as they provide a range of features and tools that simplify development and deployment. In this answer, we will discuss some of the key challenges and best practices for migrating legacy monolithic applications to microservices architecture using Spring Boot and Spring Cloud.

Challenges:

1. Decomposition: One of the main challenges in migrating a monolithic application to microservices is decomposing the monolith into smaller, independently deployable services. This requires careful planning and architecture design, as the services must be aligned with the organization's business goals and requirements.

2. Data Management: Managing data in a microservices architecture is a complex task. In a monolithic application, the data is usually stored in a centralized database, but in microservices, data may be distributed across multiple databases, making it difficult to manage and maintain consistency.

3. Testing: Testing microservices requires a different approach

from testing monolithic applications. Due to the distributed nature of microservices and their interdependencies, testing must cover not only the individual services but also the interactions between them.

4. Security: Securing a microservices architecture can be challenging, especially since each service may have its own authentication and authorization mechanisms. This requires careful planning and implementation to ensure that the whole system is secure and compliant with organizational security policies.

Best Practices for Migrating Monolithic Applications to Microservices Architecture:

1. Identify Service Boundaries: Identify the boundaries of your monolithic application to identify the individual services that must be developed. Analyze the dependencies between modules and functions to figure out the logical boundaries of each service.

2. Develop Each Service Independently: Each service must be developed and deployed independently, so it is essential to establish an appropriate DevOps environment with Continuous Integration and Continuous Deployment.

3. Use Domain Driven Design: Utilize domain-driven design (DDD) to define each service's domain accurately, making it simpler to understand their responsibilities and interconnectivity.

4. Use API Gateways: Use an API gateway to manage communication between the microservices and the client. An API gateway streamlines access to your microservices, ensuring security and regulating traffic flow.

5. Implement Monitoring and Failure-Handling Capabilities: Use monitoring tools to monitor performance, audit logs and provide transparency into the state of the system. Implement fault tolerance and circuit breaker patterns to prevent system failures when dependent modules fail.

6. Refactor Data Management: if the data is stored in too many silos for manageable development, unifying the storage system with a database like MongoDB or Cassandra can make a significant difference in the overall system performance.

In conclusion, there are several challenges to migratory legacy applications to microservices architecture using Spring Boot and Spring Cloud. By following these best practices, you can ensure that your transition is smooth while also maintaining your legacy codebase's compatibility. Ultimately, microservices will offer better scalability, flexibility, and agility for your application.

6.18   What are the strategies for ensuring data consistency and eventual consistency in microservices architecture using Spring Cloud and other tools?

In a microservices architecture, each service has its own database, and as a result, maintaining data consistency among them can be challenging.

Here are some key strategies for ensuring data consistency and eventual consistency in microservices architecture using Spring Cloud and other tools:

1. Use a two-phase commit (2PC): Two-phase commit (2PC) is a transaction protocol that ensures atomicity and consistency across multiple distributed databases involved in a distributed transaction. In this protocol, one service acts as the Coordinator and sends a prepare message to all the Participants so that they can prepare themselves accordingly. Once all participants have sent ready messages, the Coordinator sends a commit message to all participants, which results in a commit or rollback operation.

2. Implement event-driven architecture: This approach involves using events to notify other services about changes in data. When a service changes data, it can broadcast an event that other services can listen to, and make necessary adjustments in their own databases.

For example, in Spring Cloud, you can use Spring Cloud Stream to implement a message-driven architecture, where messages can be routed through an intermediate message broker such as RabbitMQ or Apache Kafka.

3. Use eventual consistency: In a distributed system, it is impossible to maintain real-time consistency. So, instead of trying to maintain consistency at all times, it's often better to aim for eventual consistency. This means that at some point in time, all services will be consistent with each other, although there might be some lag.

For example, in Spring Cloud, you can use Spring Cloud Data Flow and Spring Cloud Task to implement a batch processing system that runs periodically and updates data across multiple microservices.

4. Implement saga pattern: When a set of microservices need

to complete a business transaction that spans across multiple microservices, we can use Saga Pattern. In Saga Pattern, the microservices interact with each other and maintain a log to track the changes made. If any step in the transaction fails, the saga can be reverted back to its original state.

For example, in Spring Cloud, we can use Spring Cloud State Machine or Axon Framework to implement Saga Pattern.

In conclusion, there is no single strategy for ensuring data consistency and eventual consistency in microservices architecture using Spring Cloud and other tools. We need to choose the strategy based on the business requirements and constraints of the system.

6.19   Explain the role of Spring Cloud Function in creating serverless applications and how it integrates with various Function-as-a-Service (FaaS) platforms.

Spring Cloud Function is an open source framework that helps in creating and deploying functions in a serverless architecture. It provides a programming model for building serverless functions that can be executed in a Function-as-a-Service (FaaS) platform like AWS Lambda, Azure Functions, Google Cloud Functions, etc.

The primary role of Spring Cloud Function is to abstract away the underlying infrastructure and allow developers to focus on writing business logic. This means that the developers can write their code in a language they are comfortable with (e.g., Java, Kotlin, Groovy, etc.) and deploy it to a FaaS platform without worrying about the specific implementation details of the platform.

Spring Cloud Function provides a simple programming model based on functions. Instead of defining a class with methods, developers define individual functions and annotate them with @FunctionName to give them a unique name. These functions can be written with inputs and outputs that match the expected input and output of the FaaS platform. For example, if using AWS Lambda, developers can define a function that takes an input of type InputStream and produces an output of type OutputStream.

Spring Cloud Function provides integrations with various FaaS platforms through the use of function bindings. A function binding is a connection between a function and an event source, such as an HTTP request, an SQS queue, or an S3 bucket. Each FaaS platform has its own set of supported event sources, and Spring Cloud Function provides a set of binding implementations that map to those event sources.

For example, to deploy a Spring Cloud Function to AWS Lambda, the developer would create a new Lambda function in the AWS Console and configure it to use the Spring Cloud Function handler. The handler is responsible for invoking the correct Spring Cloud Function based on the event source. The binding for the event source can be configured using properties in the application.properties file.

In summary, Spring Cloud Function provides a convenient way to write serverless functions and deploy them to various FaaS platforms by providing a simple programming model and in-

tegrations with event sources through function bindings. It
abstracts away the underlying infrastructure and allows developers to focus on business logic, resulting in faster development
and deployment of serverless applications.

6.20   Discuss the future trends and emerg-
ing technologies in the Spring ecosystem and how they can be used for
building modern, scalable applications.

The Spring ecosystem has been constantly evolving and improving over the years, and a number of emerging technologies and
trends are poised to shape its future. Here are some notable
ones:

1. Cloud Native Computing: Cloud native computing and microservices architectures are becoming increasingly popular for
building scalable, resilient, and portable applications. To cater
to this trend, Spring has built robust support for Kubernetes,
Istio, and other cloud native technologies, allowing developers
to build and deploy cloud native applications at scale.

2. Reactive Programming: Reactive programming is gaining
traction due to its ability to handle high-throughput, low-latency,
and event-driven applications. Spring has embraced Reactive
programming with the release of the Spring WebFlux module,
which provides a fully reactive programming model, allowing for
non-blocking I/O, backpressure, and efficient use of resources.

3. Serverless Computing: Serverless computing is rapidly changing the way applications are developed and deployed by en-

abling developers to focus on code instead of infrastructure. As part of its commitment to supporting modern deployment models, Spring has built integration support for AWS Lambda, Azure Functions, and Google Cloud Functions, and has also developed the Spring Cloud Function project to facilitate serverless development.

4. AI and Machine Learning: Artificial intelligence and machine learning are emerging as key technologies for building intelligent applications that can learn from data and make intelligent decisions. Spring has developed the Spring Cloud Stream project, which enables developers to build event-driven microservices that can analyze real-time data in a scalable and efficient manner.

5. Blockchain: Blockchain is gaining ground as a disruptive technology that allows for secure and transparent transactions. Spring has responded to this trend by developing the Spring Blockchain project, which provides a framework for building blockchain-based applications using the Spring Boot and Spring Cloud projects.

In summary, the Spring ecosystem is constantly evolving and adapting to emerging technologies and trends. By embracing cloud-native computing, reactive programming, serverless computing, AI and machine learning, and blockchain, developers can leverage the power of Spring to build modern, scalable, and intelligent applications.

www.ingramcontent.com/pod-product-compliance
Lightning Source LLC
LaVergne TN
LVHW051326050326
832903LV00031B/3387